Heritage Culture and Business, Kyoto Style

Craftsmanship in the Creative Economy

Heritage Culture and Business, Kyoto Style

Craftsmanship in the Creative Economy

Murayama Yuzo

Translated by
Juliet Winters Carpenter

JAPAN LIBRARY

Note to the reader: Japanese and Chinese names are written in the western style, with the given name first, except on the jacket, case, title page, and this imprint page.

Heritage Culture and Business, Kyoto Style
- Craftsmanship in the Creative Economy -
Murayama Yuzo. Translated by Juliet Winters Carpenter.

Published by Japan Publishing Industry Foundation for Culture (JPIC)
3-12 3 Kanda-Jimbocho, Chiyoda-ku, Tokyo 101-0051, Japan

First English edition: March 2019

© Murayama Yuzo 2008

English translation © Japan Publishing Industry Foundation for Culture, 2019

Originally published in Japanese under the title of *Kyoto gata bijinesu: ∂okuso to keizoku no keieijutsu* by NHK Publishing, Inc., in 2008. English rights have been arranged with the author directly.

Jacket and Cover Design: Yunosuke Kawabe
Book Design: Andrew Pothecary (itsumo music)
Production: Aki Ueda (Pont Cerise)

Printed in Japan
ISBN 97-4-86658-058-6
http://www.jpic.or.jp/japanlibrary/

Contents

•

Introduction to the English Edition   6
Prologue: Kyoto, City of Creativity   9

Chapter One: **The Culture of Craftsmanship at the**   17
Heart of Kyoto Business
     1. The Culture of Craftsmanship in Heritage Industries   18
     2. The Culture of Craftsmanship, Alive in High-tech Industry   30
Chapter Two: **Combining Tradition and Technology**   41
     1. The Influence of Heritage Industries on High-tech Industries   42
     2. The Influence of High-Tech Industries on Heritage Industries   46
Chapter Three: **Creating New Value from Cultural Capital**   55
     1. Culture Supported by the Common People   56
     2. Contemporary Value from Historical Assets   62
Chapter Four: **Keeping Cultural Businesses in Business**   71
     1. The Birth of Cultural Business   72
     2. Innovation for the Sake of Continuity   78
     3. Heritage Industries at a Crossroads   82
Chapter Five: **Culture Meets Culture**   89
     1. Collaborations that Shatter Tradition   90
     2. Linking Kyoto and Overseas Cultures   101
Chapter Six: **Kyoto Culture Goes Global**   111
     1. Kyoto Culture Promoted from the Outside   112
     2. Global Development Using Traditional Materials   114
     3. Conveying the Heart of Kyoto Culture to the World   119
Chapter Seven: **The Creative Economy of Kyoto: Implications**   131
     1. People-centric Creativity   132
     2. Cultural Business as a Part of Daily Life   136
     3. Craftsmanship and Technology in the Age of Culture   144

Bibliograhy   151
About the Author and the Translator   159

•

Introduction to the English Edition

KYOTO HAS MANY BUSINESSES THAT PREDATE THE FOUNDING OF THE UNITED States. Of those introduced in this book, Shoyeido was founded 314 years ago; Hosoo, a traditional kimono textile maker, was founded 331 years ago; and the restaurant Hyotei goes back some 400 years. Venerable family-owned enterprises such as these are maintained by making culture their business—a method of preserving historical culture that is rare in the world. The chance to experience living traditional culture as a part of daily life gives sightseeing in Kyoto inimitable appeal.

Traditional culture and business have developed in Kyoto while maintaining a delicate balance, one backed by a set of business principles and a mentality that are unique to the ancient capital. Kyoto business practices are nothing like the US-style emphasis on rationality and efficiency, but have a depth and consistency nurtured over centuries. Not only managers of culture-related businesses but also those of high-tech companies such as Shimadzu Corporation, Kyocera, and Horiba subscribe to these principles and values. They are the source of Kyoto companies' strong global competitiveness.

The principles and mentality that imbue Kyoto's business world are so taken for granted by locals that little explanation has been offered to the outside world until now. Perhaps this is a symptom of what many Japanese denigrate as Kyoto exclusivity. However, those principles and that mentality—Kyoto business practices, in short—are chock full of managerial wisdom developed through the ages. This book is intended to fill a longstanding gap by conveying them to as wide an audience as possible.

The English version is based on a book I wrote ten years ago called *Kyoto-gata bijinesu: Dokuso to keizoku no keieijutsu* (Kyoto-style business: The art of management encouraging originality and continuity). While maintaining the essence of the Japanese original, it includes many more photographs of heritage industries, along with annotations and explanations to aid in readers' understanding. Also, by adding information on the latest trends, I have tried to convey a sense of immediacy in the portrayal of innovations to traditional Kyoto culture. The English version accordingly differs considerably from the Japanese original.

I was fortunate to have the book translated by Professor Juliet Carpenter of Doshisha Women's College, an expert translator and longtime Kyoto resident with deep knowledge of the city. In particular, her translation perfectly captures the voices of craftspeople and managers concerning the essence of Kyoto culture. Also, her office is close to mine, and we were able to meet in person several times to discuss the translation, an experience I enjoyed very much. I am deeply grateful to her.

In the early seventeenth century, gorgeous editions of classical literature known as *sagabon* were published in Kyoto, integrating calligraphy and artwork. In that spirit, I wanted this book to be not just another business book but to incorporate aspects of art in a profoundly beautiful way. For their acceptance of my idea and their efforts to make it a reality, I would like to express my sincere gratitude to Kiyoshi Nakaizumi, Izumi Ozaki, and Rico Komanoya of Japan Publishing Industry Foundation for Culture.

Murayama Yuzo
February 2019

Sagabon, *gorgeous editions of classical literature, were products of collaboration between calligrapher Hon'ami Koetsu, painter Tawaraya Sotatsu, and the wealthy merchant Suminokura Soan, leading men of culture in early 17th-century Kyoto. Pictured above is part of the handscroll "Anthology with Crane Design," which came about through this collaboration. Today, in a different form, Kyoto retains the link between traditional culture and business spirit that gave rise to such works.*
Photo: Kyoto National Museum

Prologue

•

Kyoto, City of Creativity

KYOTO IS HOME TO MANY UNIQUE BUSINESSES. NINTENDO, BY COMING OUT with creative gaming devices like the Nintendo Switch and Wii, has remained at the forefront of the worldwide video game industry. Kyocera has attracted wide attention not only for its specialty—electronics—but also for its innovative Amoeba Management method. Omron developed its fundamental philosophy of "working for the benefit of society" as far back as the 1950s, and it continues to be a leading proponent of corporate social responsibility in Japan. The venture firm Horiba, whose company motto is "Joy and Fun," has carved out a unique niche by developing products and equipment in fields such as environmental monitoring. Nidec Corporation became the world's number one manufacturer of comprehensive motors with a growth strategy that effectively utilizes mergers and acquisitions, while Shimadzu Corporation gave rise to Japan's sole Nobel laureate from the business world. Other exceptional Kyoto businesses include Murata Manufacturing, Screen Holdings, Rohm, Ishida, and many more.

At the same time, Kyoto is home to living heritage industries. Beginning with *yuzen* dyeing, Nishijin silk weaving, and other industries affiliated with the making of kimono, there are Kiyomizuyaki, Rakuyaki, and other styles of ceramics, as well as the manufacture of incense, lacquerware, folding and round fans, dolls, woodblock prints, cuisine, and many more. No other city embodies Japan's traditional culture the way Kyoto does. Long-established shops supporting these multiform aspects of Japanese tradition and culture continue to thrive, many of them founded two or three hundred years ago. Indeed, of the more than 1,900 companies in Kyoto Prefecture that have been in business for at least a century, the majority are clustered in Kyoto City. This figure is one of the highest in Japan, a country noted for the longevity of its business enterprises, and it shows the remarkable staying power of Kyoto businesses.

How did Kyoto become a city like no other, one where unique cutting-edge businesses coexist with traditional culture?

Kyoto's Culture of Craftsmanship

"Creativity" and "continuity" are key words in the search for an explanation of Kyoto's identity as a center of businesses both old and new. Probing deeper into the city's essential nature requires familiarity with the long tradition of craftsmanship it has nurtured—what I refer to as Kyoto's "culture of craftsmanship." Later I will take this up in some detail, but broadly speaking, it has three components.

First is *face-to-face management and constant improvement in friendly rivalry*.[1] Taking a systematic approach to managing workers is generally frowned upon in Kyoto, and in most companies, management deals with workers face-to-face. This human-oriented style of management is paired with an atmosphere where workers polish their skills through rigorous discipline, friendly rivalry, and mutual encouragement. This tendency is particularly strong in heritage industries such as *yuzen* dyeing and Nishijin silk weaving, where assorted craftspeople form a network in which constant refinement of skills is required. Steady improvement in a spirit of friendly rivalry has made possible the extraordinary level of specialization and craftsmanship required to create Kyoto's exquisite kimono.

The second component is *providing added value through creativity*. One thing Kyotoites dislike is imitating others. This means that they devote great energy to the pursuit of creativity and seek by that means to increase the added value of what they make. Kyoto businesses attach importance to maintaining an appropriate scale: rather than immoderate expansion, they seek growth through enhanced creativity.

Third, Kyoto's culture of craftsmanship is characterized by *innovation for the sake of continuity*. The ancient capital is often described as a place of innovation amid tradition. While this is certainly true, the efforts of traditional enterprises to engage in innovation stem less from a desire for profit-making than from a determination to stay in business. Establishments that have been around for two or three centuries know their priority is not immediate profits but handing the business over intact to the next generation. Kyoto businesses deservedly enjoy a reputation for innovation, but it must be remembered that their efforts differ from the norm in one important way: they innovate to survive.

The Creative Class and Urban Prosperity

Richard Florida, a professor of Business and Creativity at the Rotman School of Management, University of Toronto, believes that urban prosperity hinges on what he calls the "creative class." He includes in this category artists, musicians, architects, scientists, designers, and all other knowledge-based professionals, whose collective creativity he sees as the prime resource for economic development today. According to him, economic competitiveness depends on elevating individual creativity, and cities' economic growth depends on attracting and nurturing a talented population.

Crucially, Florida emphasizes not cutting-edge technology per se but the people who devise it. This idea ties in with the first characteristic of Kyoto's culture of craftsmanship, the people-centric approach to management and constant polishing of skills in a spirit of friendly rivalry. Florida's theory is premised on human mobility amid rising competition for the creative class among cities around the world, yet Kyoto is an example of a city where creativity has been maximized through a unique system of management.

Florida further expounds on the city as the key economic and social unit of our time. While globalization has normalized economic trading across national borders, the city is where diverse economic forces come together.

The city of Kyoto, as is often pointed out, displays insular tendencies. Its very insularity, however, means that the city is well integrated, enhancing its potential as a unit of economic prosperity. Florida's fundamental insight is that we are now seeing a shift from the old production system, where products are manufactured from raw materials, to a creative economy constrained only by the limits of human talent and imagination. Cities adapting to this scenario will prosper. Its dual attributes of creativity and continuity give rise to a new image of Kyoto as a creative city in Florida's sense.

John Howkins, a leading expert on the creative economy, has served as consultant to Time Warner, IBM, and many other top companies and institutions. He has also served as special management advisor to governments in the United States, Europe, and Japan. His analysis of the creative economy is based on fifteen sectors including art, music, film, fashion, and publishing. Hawkins makes the point that creative industries all involve intellectual property. This perspective underscores the significance of Kyoto's greatest intellectual property—the wealth of traditional knowledge accumulated down the centuries by heritage industries. Kyoto's true strength lies in this cultural capital, which continues even now to give rise to new businesses. As will be shown, Kyocera, Murata Manufacturing, and other cutting-edge firms are outgrowths of Kyoto's cultural capital with links to heritage industries.

The Organization of This Book

Kyoto is a city where a cluster of unique businesses have long supported creativity and continuity backed by history and culture. The thinking and policies that have created this dynamic business environment will be explored in the succeeding chapters.

Chapter 1 explores the nature of Kyoto's culture of craftsmanship from a business perspective. One interesting thing about Kyoto is that the world of traditional craftspeople carries over into high-tech industries on the cutting edge of innovation. Chapter 2 builds on this discussion, focusing on how traditional culture is enmeshed with technology in Kyoto and how it has helped to form the city's business climate. Chapter 3 then explores the mechanisms by which Kyoto's cultural capital—its other major characteristic and strength—gives rise to new businesses.

Chapter 4 looks back through history to verify how culture-based businesses came into being in Kyoto and how they have been maintained. Heritage industries today are then placed in the context of this historical process, with a consideration of the perils they now face. The next two chapters take up the innovative developments taken to meet these challenges, showing concrete ways that businesses are grappling with the problems of today. Chapter 5 deals with a variety of collaborative initiatives being taken within and across industries, and Chapter 6 focuses on how heritage industries are responding to globalization.

The final chapter closely examines the special nature of Kyoto's creative cultural businesses from the three perspectives of people-centric creativity; cultural business, where culture is part of daily life; and the fusion of tradition and technology. From this analysis emerges a vision for the future of the Japanese economy.

Voices from the Field

In writing this book, I wanted to highlight the people who are companies' greatest assets and incorporate their comments directly into the text. To that end, I spoke at length with managers of numerous high-tech and heritage industries and, above all, with craftspeople.

Since joining the faculty of Doshisha Business School, I have been entrusted with work relating to Kyoto, and I have enjoyed the opportunity of holding discussions with a great many people. In my capacity as advisor to the Kyoto Association of Corporate Executives, whose roster includes the city's top business leaders, I have participated in discussions of Kyoto's heritage industries and cultural businesses. In addition, I am a member of a study group set up to consider "Wisdom Business," a vision for Kyoto advanced in 2008 by Yoshio Tateishi, former Omron CEO and Chairman of the Kyoto Chamber of Commerce and Industry. I have also been granted the opportunity of participating in regular meetings held by the owners of Kyoto's famous *ryotei*, high-class Japanese restaurants. Late at night, over delicious meals of Kyoto cuisine, I have been afforded a rare glimpse into the unique world of Kyoto's top chefs.

Meanwhile, at Doshisha Business School, from 2007 to 2016 I headed a program called Kakushin Juku ("Innovation Academy") aimed at promoting the innovative globalization of Kyoto's heritage industries. Classes were designed to train young managers in those industries, but experienced managers grappling with the challenges of innovation also joined in, and discussions were invariably stimulating. My graduate seminar also attracted an assortment of students not typically seen in business school: those pursuing careers in the fields of incense, *yuzen* dyeing, ceramics, cuisine, ikebana, and other traditional arts and crafts of Kyoto. Here, too, challenges facing Kyoto's heritage industries and possibilities for future development were debated with passion. In this way, I steadily deepened my ties with representatives of Kyoto's heritage industries.

The Family Business of Nishijin Weaving and an Outsider's Perspective

My own field of study is economic security, a branch of international political economy. In the course of my career, besides organizing academic conferences on related topics, I have served on committees established by the Ministry of Economy, Trade and Industry and the Ministry of Defense. Before joining Doshisha, I was a securities analyst for Nomura Research Institute and also researched high-tech industries in Europe and the United States. My professional background thus has no connection to Kyoto's heritage industries.

What then enables me to write a book on a topic such as this? The answer is simple: I was born in Kyoto's Nishijin district. Nishijin silk weaving was my family's business, and when I was a child weavers were constantly in and out of our house. My father worked his way up to vice-president of a major

Nishijin textile firm and devoted himself to innovation. Accordingly, when I speak with people who manage or work for heritage firms, I am able to pick up on the hidden nuances of what is said. My family background was a great boon in researching and writing this book, which combines the subjectivity of a native Kyotoite with the objectivity of an academic researcher.

Indeed, my goal was not to write as an insider, looking inward as so many previous books on Kyoto have done, but to take a wider view, examining the business lessons that the rest of Japan and countries around the world can draw from Kyoto's rich experience.

Prologue notes

1. From the Japanese phrase *sessa takuma* ["cut the stone, polish the gem"], referring to self-improvement through meticulous discipline and the rough and tumble of working in friendly rivalry with others.

•

The Culture of Craftsmanship at the Heart of Kyoto Business

THIS CHAPTER TAKES A CLOSER LOOK AT THREE FORMATIVE ELEMENTS OF THE culture of Kyoto craftsmanship: (1) combining face-to-face management practices with constant improvement in an atmosphere of friendly rivalry; (2) providing added value through creativity; and (3) innovating for the sake of continuity. Furthermore, the chapter will examine how the culture of craftsmanship affects not only traditional businesses but management practices in high-tech industries, thereby giving Kyoto businesses a distinct competitive edge.

1. The Culture of Craftsmanship in Heritage Industries

Production Networks of Heritage Industries

To understand the mechanism of business in Kyoto, it is essential to begin by looking at how traditional crafts are manufactured. Division of labor is the foundation of Kyoto's heritage industries. *Yuzen* hand-dyeing, for example, involves as many as fifteen to twenty steps, each carried out by a different set of specialists, from designing the pattern and preparing the white silk cloth to sketching in the design, tracing its outlines with a paste-resist, applying dye, steaming the cloth to fasten the dye, rinsing out excess starch and dye, drying the cloth, and finally smoothing out wrinkles. The division of labor is organized by a sort of producer known as a *shikkaiya*. *(See photo 1, opposite.)*

A similar approach is involved in Nishijin silk weaving. Kyoto folding fans and Kiyomizu ceramics were also, at least until the 1970s, produced by a comparable division of labor. In this way, traditional industry in Kyoto is characterized by production systems that are based on artisan networks, the skills of each individual combining to produce works of the finest quality.

Polishing Skills in Friendly Rivalry

Unlike other areas of Japan, in Kyoto each network of artisans is relatively fixed, there being few itinerant craftspeople and jacks-of-all-trades. As most artisans follow in the family tradition, labor mobility is low. Members of the same network hone and polish their skills in an atmosphere of friendly rivalry, encouraging one another to constantly improve. If the skills of even one member of the chain are sub-par, the finished product will suffer in quality, so the various workers all encourage one another to keep standards high.

Photo 1: *Applying colors: one step in the yuzen dyeing process. The craftsperson carefully mixes dyes to create the best colors and painstakingly applies them by hand.*

Photo: Tomihiro Hand-Dyeing Yuzen Co., Ltd.

Still, there may be lingering doubt as to the efficiency of such a system. I once had the opportunity to discuss this with an old friend who was born into a school of Noh *taiko* drummers and took over as head in his turn. Just back from the United States, where I had been taught the efficiency of American-style free competition, I posed the following questions: "Having to follow a certain line of work just because you happened to be born into a certain family doesn't allow everyone to do their best work, does it? What if your child turns out to be a dunce with no aptitude for drumming? What will you do?" My friend explained, "Even a dunce is bound to become better than average at drumming if he's exposed to the sound from an early age and allowed to handle the *taiko*." In other words, those who are surrounded by drummers from infancy can, in an atmosphere of constant striving and encouragement, rise above the ordinary. Herein lies the secret of true craftsmanship.

In Kyoto, interpersonal relationships serve to foster precisely this sort of atmosphere. Yoshihiro Murata, the third-generation owner and chef of the renowned Kikunoi restaurant, has led innovation in Japanese cuisine and made a name for himself internationally. Here is what he has to say about the world of Kyoto chefs:

Kyoto chefs are like a family. You never know when you might need one of them to do something for you. It's really a monolithic world. In one book I refer to it as 'Kyoto Cuisine, Inc.'

People that my father looked after when he ran the restaurant went on to acquire senior status, and then it was their turn to teach me things. Sometimes it's easier to absorb lessons from somebody you're not related to than it is to be lectured by your own father. And now I teach things to the children of people I'm indebted to. A similar web of relationships exists throughout Kyoto.

From the time I was a boy, I used to get lectured by the owners of other establishments: 'What got into you?' they'd say. 'What made you do that?' A lot of them were extraordinary men, larger than life, and hearing that kind of talk from them made more of an impression on me than hearing it from my own father. Now it's my turn to grab other people's children and younger chefs and sit them down for a talking-to. I fully expect that someday they'll do the same for my son when he needs it—and my grandson too.

No one thinks, 'Only our lot should improve.' Everyone in the restaurant business in Kyoto realizes that wouldn't work. The thinking is rather, 'We're all in this together; why not all improve together?' Others may see that as a kind of Kyoto exclusiveness. But we offer wholehearted support not only to restaurants we have a long history with, but also to those started up by children of people we've trained.[1]

Face-to-Face Management

The system of constant improvement in friendly rivalry is human-oriented and works only if the people involved continually strive to polish their skills. To properly manage a network of such workers and come up with fine products, the manager must deal with each worker individually, face-to-face.

Takeshi Shinmura is vice president of Ganko Food Service, which runs a unique chain of restaurants including Nijoen, set in the former villa of Kyoto magnate Suminokura Ryoi (1554–1614), the creator of Takasegawa Canal. Shinmura supervises the company chefs and has said this about his job:

We employ a lot of chefs, and managing them is basically a hands-on job. I sit down and chat periodically with each one, picking up on their awareness of issues, their goals, and so forth. By listening to them at work or going out for drinks together after hours, I get a sense of their thinking as I seek to strike a balance between efficient management and workers' needs. Bearing down on chefs only gets their dander up; you have to give them a certain amount of lee-

way to cook as they please. It doesn't work unless you create an atmosphere where they think, 'If he says so, I'll go along with it.'[2]

Increasing Added Value through an Emphasis on Individuality

Managing craftspeople with various peculiarities and quirks requires personal, face-to-face interaction. This approach places limits on the number of workers that can be successfully managed. The impracticality of expanding the human-oriented system of workers into a mass production system makes it difficult to come up with a growth model based on quantitative expansion. The only way to create a profit while staying relatively small in scale is to aim for higher profitability. However, steps to improve efficiency and hold down costs can only go so far. Because the handiwork of artisans is manual by definition, pursuit of full mechanization with an eye to improving efficiency can lower costs only at the expense of the distinctive flavor that makes an artisan's work so valuable.

Accordingly, Kyoto's artisan system can only increase its added value by refining workers' skills. The goal is to increase added value by enhancing their individuality and uniqueness, their distinctive flavor and characteristic quirks. Keeping the workers within eyeshot of the manager also makes possible quality control. These points, along with steady improvement in an atmosphere of friendly rivalry, define the Kyoto artisan system.

Concerning the distinctive flavor and quirks of an artisan, here are the comments of Hirokazu Kato, a ceramic artist who has studied in Italy as well as Japan and who has won numerous awards for his work, mainly in celadon and white porcelain:

> *I think what distinguishes Kyoto ceramics is the attention paid to the potter's individuality, the priority given to individuality instead of mass production. This is different from ceramics elsewhere, I believe. Kyoto hasn't got an abundance of fine-quality clay, and resources are limited, so potters have to do what they can to increase the value of the finished product. For example, if someone tells a potter who makes Mino ware, 'Raise this a centimeter,' he has to make a prototype, then a mold, and a whole line, so his answer is, 'How many are you going to order? We do a thousand per lot.' But in Kyoto, he'll say, 'Well now, this is Kyoto, so the cost per item will be a little high, but I can make you ten at a time.' Japanese pottery is something you hold in your hand, so this*

is really important, it seems to me.

Something else I find interesting about Kyoto pottery is that potters make small items based on a sudden idea. Even at a higher cost per item, they'll make small batches of little items, really unusual ones with a lot of variance. Kyoto potters have no trouble adapting.[3] (See photo 2, left.)

Photo 2: Blue and white celadon dishes by Hirokazu Kato. Beauty born of painstaking experimentation and the rich experience of a seasoned craftsman. Photo: Hirokazu Kato

What Kato is describing applies to the city's heritage industries in general. Kyoto craftspeople have overcome the scarcity of natural resources by using their wits and overlaying their work with cultural value. Uji tea from Kyoto Prefecture, for example, is famous throughout the country, yet the amount of unprocessed tea produced in the prefecture is a mere 4 percent of the national total. Uji tea has achieved fame despite these circumstances because growers strive to increase added value by specializing in high-quality tea and by taking full advantage of the superior blending techniques developed through history.

Products' Dual Nature

From an economic perspective, the distinctiveness of Kyoto products inevitably comes down to their dual nature. According to economic theory, consumers purchase something because it is of use to them, and therefore it provides them with satisfaction. Consumers' actual psychology, however, is a bit more complex. Someone purchasing an automobile, for example, will consider a variety of factors. In addition to basics like performance, mileage, and operability, the buyer will pay attention to design and safety. In buying a hybrid car, environmental impact will be a factor. In other words, the buyer considers not only the functional, "hard" aspects of the product, but its special "soft" qualities as well, at times willingly paying extra for the latter.

The products of Nishijin silk weaving, *yuzen* dyeing, and other traditional Kyoto crafts with a cultural dimension are classic examples of products with desirable "soft" qualities. The purchaser of a kimono made by traditional methods pays not only for the functionality of the garment but for its attendant cultural value. In the final analysis, such cultural value takes us into the realm of art. The painted folding screens of Ogata Korin (1658–1716), for example, or the works of the seventeenth-century potter Nonomura Ninsei (dates of birth and death unknown) are valued not for their functionality but exclusively for their cultural and artistic attributes. Products that people buy thus range from the supremely functional, like hand soap and toothbrushes, to items appreciated for their cultural value, like works of fine art, with the majority falling somewhere between.

Yoshihiro Murata describes this dual nature in the context of his high-end restaurant, Kikunoi:

> *As a cook, I believe that my customer's main goal is to enjoy a meal. But even an inexpensive bowl of noodles can be really satisfying, so I have to ask myself why people bother coming to my restaurant. It seems to me that they come to purchase not food but time, that my restaurant is part of the leisure industry, a living museum. Otherwise, there are just too many things that don't add up from the customer's point of view. I could reduce floor space to save money and charge less for the food I serve, but even if the dishes maintained the same quality, would customers be more satisfied and increase their patronage? The answer is no.*[4]

Balancing Business and Culture

It is fair to say that Kyoto craftspeople succeed in business not only because of the functionality of the things they make, but also because their products' enhanced cultural significance raises their added value. Capable workers and managers in Kyoto are keenly aware of the need to balance functionality and culture. Laying too much emphasis on the one leads to price wars, with diminished profitability, while excessive attention to the other pushes them into the realm of art, at the expense of market size.

To succeed in business with a product that has significant cultural value, craftspeople and managers must cultivate a sense of balance.

Not all Kyoto businesses are built on the same sense of balance, however. Different industries have their own standards and knowhow. Once, in conversation with a Nishijin silk weaver who has collaborated with an Italian designer, wishing to assess the relative weight of business and culture in his work, I asked, "Do you deal in culture?" He replied in the affirmative. But on another occasion when I put the same question to the manager of a large tea-processing industry, he said, "No, I deal *alongside* culture." And the manager of a major incense company in Kyoto responded, "Culture itself does the dealing."

From these short answers, I think the reader can gather that the incense manufacturer's comment shows the greatest consideration for the cultural aspect of what he does, while the Nishijin weaver shows the greatest consideration for the business aspect of his work. In this way, Kyoto managers all have a different sense of the proper balance between the two. Finding the right balance and integrating it into one's management method is the key to successfully incorporating culture into one's business.

Innovation for the Sake of Continuity

As described above, Kyoto businesspeople increase the added value of their product by incorporating its cultural significance. What complicates the matter is that culture is in constant flux, changing with the times. A *yuzen*-dyed kimono was the height of fashion in the Genroku era (1688–1704), but today such kimono no longer have a high-fashion image and their relative market share is small. As lifestyles have changed over the centuries, people's impressions of *yuzen*-dyed kimonos have changed accordingly.

Unless a business can adapt to such changes over time, the culture it is promoting will be out of sync with the era. Such a situation cries out for innovation. Thus, to incorporate culture into one's business and keep it going, the cultural value attached to the product must adapt to the times. This is the meaning of "innovation" in the context of Kyoto's heritage industries. In the world of Kyoto craftspeople, the word does not imply radical transformation but offers rather a means of promoting stability and continuity. This is why we speak of "innovation for the sake of continuity." Says Kikunoi's Murata:

What my predecessor taught me was 'always be aware of your mission as a cook,' which is to present dishes that will ensure customer satisfaction in each successive era. It's not enough to say, 'We've always done it this way, so we'll go on preparing food the same way in the future.' Unlike a hundred years ago, Japanese people today are accustomed to French and Italian cuisine and may not be satisfied with an old recipe. People's sense of flavor is constantly evolving. There are techniques for making and presenting food as if that weren't so. When offering something new, it's important not to make an issue of how different it is, but to present it as something perfectly normal. You want an eighty-year-old woman to say, 'I've never tasted anything like this before, but it's good.' What you don't want is for her to ask herself before she tries it, 'Is this Japanese-style food, or not?' You need to keep that line in mind and not cross it, so that what you're serving doesn't strike your customers as strange.[5]

Computer Graphics *Yuzen* and the Meaning of Innovation

Entrepreneur Yunosuke Kawabe once gave a lecture explaining the innovative technique of using computer graphics to produce traditional patterns handed down within the Kawabe family for use in swimsuits and interior design. *(See photo 3, overleaf.)* Afterward, a member of the audience affiliated with Hagi ware kilns pointed out that improvements in distribution have made it possible to obtain all sorts of clay and fuel, so that Bizen ware could be produced in Hagi, to use an extreme example. There is a strong possibility that some new form of Hagi pottery will be developed and made into a business, but in that case, he wanted to know, could the new product truly be called "Hagi ware"? Would Hagi ware in fact disappear along with the culture surrounding it?

This question gets to the heart of the matter. For Kawabe, who by developing CG *yuzen* is apparently parting company with traditional hand-painted *yuzen* techniques, it was particularly relevant. He responded with his personal view that when tradition becomes stifling, it impedes survival. He then gave his take on innovation:

In Kyoto, tradition has constantly evolved. The word 'tradition' makes people feel that a certain way of doing things must not be changed, but in fact over time people have made all sorts of changes for the sake of their business, as well they should. The question is how you approach doing such a thing. The best approach is to maintain tradition while incorporating change, not to hold on to it in form only; if tradition is passed on as culture, it seems to me the form can change.[6]

Someone asked, "After all the success CG *yuzen* has had, would it pain you if someone told you that what you're making isn't *yuzen*?" He replied, "Not in the least. *Yuzen* is becoming something new." Subsequently, Kawabe told me he saw himself returning to hand-painted *yuzen* in old age—a reminder of the living, unchanging core of Kyoto culture.

Kawabe also told me about the time he paid a visit to the former studio of artist Inagaki Toshijiro (1902–1963), who was designated a Living National Treasure for his kimono stencil patterns, and a family member showed him Inagaki's sketchbook. Seeing that sketchbook in the very room where Inagaki did his sketching made him feel able to communicate with the master. He saw how sunlight came in from the garden, for example, and clearly sensed how Inagaki had rendered that on paper. It occurred to him then that the sort of shared understanding that he felt with a fellow *yuzen* dye

Photo 3: CG Yuzen by Yunosuke Kawabe. He divided the creative process into design and manufacturing and used digital technology for the latter, thereby widening the application and lowering production cost. Photo: Yunosuke Kawabe

artist was in itself a form of culture.

It is precisely because Kawabe has this awareness that he can pursue CG *yuzen* without remorse. Innovation requires the ability to cherish and maintain the core of culture, and the courage to cast aside what is unnecessary.

Cultural Core

What is the core of Kyoto's culture of craftsmanship? Explaining this to anyone who did not grow up in a Kyoto heritage industry is not easy. One way to think of it is the sensibility of a true professional. Over time, devoted workers who take professional pride in their work acquire an intuitive ability based on their accumulated knowledge, training, and experience. Such an internal hidden sense is what I refer to as the "core," and in the case of a Kyoto artisan, it is based not on the length of one lifetime but on the accumulated experience of five or ten generations. Someone living in such an environment cannot help but become imbued with the culture of craftsmanship. That culture also permeates the world of kyogen, an ancient form of comic theater that evolved alongside Noh.

Akira Shigeyama is the son of innovative kyogen master Sennojo Shigeyama (1923–2010) and head of a kyogen lineage going back over two hundred fifty years. Like his father before him, he has experimented with new forms of the classical comic theater. After coming up with such unconventional ideas as "science-fiction kyogen" and collaborating with overseas artists to find new modes of expression, in the end he came to the surprising realization that "kyogen was all I had." *(See photo 4, overleaf.)* While sharing the stage with actors overseas, he realized that his way of standing, for example, was different from theirs; he alone used the kyogen-style way of standing in a stable posture with the knees slightly bent. As he put it,

> *Through trying new things, I came to see that as an actor, all I was capable of was kyogen. Everything I did ended up being kyogen. I first went on stage at the age of two and a half, so I've been performing kyogen for nearly half a century. I don't think there's anything inside me now but kyogen.*[7]

In the space of fifty years, something in kyogen became an indelible part of Akira Shigeyama. Try as he may, he cannot shed it. This sense is what I mean by a cultural "core." Even if the outward form changes, the

Photo 4: Akira Shigeyama performing with innovative NOHO Theater Group. Against simple costumes and setting, his kyogen-style performance is powerful.

Photo: NOHO Theater Group

core remains constant. This concept offers a glimpse of how Kyoto culture has endured. *(See photo 5, opposite.)*

Long-term Perspective and Preference for Authenticity

Kyoto managers and craftspeople may adapt somewhat to the times, but there is nothing they dislike more than being swept or carried away by change. This tendency also points to an underlying sensibility akin to the cultural core that makes long-term survival possible.

During Japan's economic bubble, restaurateur Yoshihiro Murata considered raising prices and consulted with his father, whose advice was "Wait five years. Five years after you have an idea like that, you'll be able to see clearly which way society is headed." Once a restaurant raises prices, it's hard to go back, and since the bubble eventually burst, wreaking havoc, resisting the temptation to pursue short-term profit was clearly the right choice. Kyotoites are in business for the long haul. The tendency to resist being swept up by short-term phenomena and to base one's actions rather on what will contribute to long-term survival is characteristic of Kyoto-style management. Says Murata:

The purpose of our work isn't to make a profit, but to stay in business. That's why we are not an industry but a family business. Our way of operating isn't to seek profits but to be fixated on staying around. Where will we be in a

hunðreð years? That's the question.
Japan has a saying, isshi soden *[transmission of traðe secrets from father to only one chilð]. For example, the restaurant Hyotei serves a ðish calleð 'Hyotei eggs,' founð nowhere else. What really neeðs to be passeð on to the next generation isn't just recipes, however, but the attituðe towarð the business. If that isn't carefully taught to whoever is next in line, the business will collapse in the next generation.*

When you think about it, the economy can't keep growing forever. Sooner or later, growth is bounð to come to a halt. I think our ancestors knew that, baseð on history. They planneð aheað, so when growth stoppeð they knew what to ðo. That thinking applies toðay.[8]

Photo 5: Akira Shigeyama performing the classic kyogen "Busu" (Delicious poison). Note the traðitional costume anð stance.
Photo: Yunosuke Kawabe

Murata points out that prioritizing the continuation of one's business makes it possible to invest in it from a long-term perspective, which also contributes to the accumulation of culture. Kikunoi uses its contacts with antique dealers to purchase valuable scroll paintings costing millions of yen—something that would be impossible if investing only for the short term. Murata has in mind the Kikunoi that his grandson will one day inherit and feels that "buying when we can will make things easier for my grandson."

This long-term perspective adds to the profundity and authenticity of Kyoto culture. Living in such an environment, moreover, trains the craftsman's eye to recognize and value authenticity. These things help to account for the depths of the Kyoto culture of craftsmanship.

2. The Culture of Craftsmanship, Alive in High-tech Industry

Integration of Artisan and Residential Areas

Another interesting aspect of the Kyoto culture of craftsmanship is that it can be seen not only in heritage industries but in the city's wider undercurrents. The managers of Kyoto's world-leading high-technology industries incorporate elements of that culture unawares. This is partly because of the unparalleled integration of Kyoto's work and residential areas.

Osamu Tsuji is the CEO, chairman, and executive officer of Samco, a vanguard company that manufactures semiconductor production equipment. He not only runs the company himself but has studied the characteristics of Kyoto-based industries, and he communicates his findings actively through articles and lectures. According to Tsuji, the leading characteristic of Kyoto is its high integration of work and residential areas.

"Kyoto is known as a city of *monozukuri*," Tsuji points out, using the Japanese term for manufacturing, which conveys a synthesis of technological savvy and the dedicated, perfectionist spirit of craftsmanship. He continues:

> *I'm often invited to join committees and informal talk sessions on* monozukuri *in the city or prefecture. What often comes up on those occasions is the fact that Kyoto* monozukuri *spans a millennium, having existed throughout the Heian, Azuchi- Momoyama, and Edo periods. Kyoto is a city of craftspeople, a city where workplaces coexist with residences. Living in Kyoto means living next door to a craftsperson or shopkeeper. Lately, zoning laws divide work and residential areas up neatly, but there is merit in mingling them, too. Kyoto is unique in that respect.*[9]

As Tsuji says, Kyoto is indeed a city where one finds oneself "living next door to a craftsperson or shopkeeper"—an environment markedly different from that of a neighborhood populated mainly by company workers and their families. Kyoto residents are accustomed from childhood to being surrounded by artisans and merchants, people inextricably identified with what they do; thus, sheer force of habit makes it mentally impossible to separate people from their work. Growing up in such an environment is completely different from growing up in the sort of neighborhood where what your neighbor (or your father, for that matter) does all day in a city office is impossible to imagine.

In Kyoto, factories of manufacturing industries as well as heritage industry workshops are located right in the city, often cheek by jowl with private
homes. The intertwining of daily life and work has enabled artisan culture
to permeate citizens' lives and thinking.

The M&A Strategy of Nidec Corporation

Under the leadership of Chairman of the Board, CEO, and founder Shigenobu Nagamori, Nidec Corporation, the world's leading manufacturer of
comprehensive motors, has developed a mergers and acquisitions strategy
bearing the hallmarks of Kyoto craftsmanship. M&A is the pillar of Nidec's
growth strategy; since its founding in 1973, the corporation has purchased
over sixty companies, something extraordinary in Japan. This growth model
may seem far removed from the Kyoto craftsmanship we have been consid-
ering. However, on close examination, the management practices involved
in Nidec's purchase and rebuilding of other companies also show the influence of the world of Kyoto crafts.

In April 2007, Nidec made a successful takeover bid for Japan Servo, a
Hitachi subsidiary. The acquisition of a subsidiary of the Japanese conglom-
erate by what was then a startup company made headlines, but Nagamori
had spent an astonishing sixteen years in preparation. Attracted by Servo's
technology, he first broached a merger to Hitachi president Katsushige
Mita in 1991. At the time, however, Nidec's net sales amounted to merely
60 billion yen, and the sale was not a viable option. Nagamori continued to
plead his case anyway, finally achieving a breakthrough with Kazuo Furu-
kawa, the third Hitachi president after Mita.[10]

This takeover technique—acquiring a company that offers desirable
technology by taking the time to patiently win it over—could not be more
different from the style of American management. Behind the slow, deliberate approach lies the Nagamori philosophy that "M&A deals are like a
romance. The suitor must always show sincerity and humility," waiting
patiently until the other party says yes. This attitude is by no means limited
to the purchase of domestic companies but applies equally to overseas pur-
chases. At the end of every year, Nagamori sends off New Year's greetings to
dozens of overseas firms. The letters are not simply conventional greetings
but a chance for him to convey a message to top management in firms with

technology he wishes to acquire: "If you have any interest in selling your company, please let me know." Through honest persistence, he manages to acquire the companies he is after. This is Nagamori-style M&A.[11]

Unlike American conglomerates, Nagamori does not conduct takeovers by short-term transactions using the power of capital; instead he takes the long view, working considerately with management and employees of the other company in a humanistic way. Nothing illustrates this approach better than the restructuring that follows a takeover.

In principle, after purchasing a company Nagamori leaves managers and workers in place and avoids layoffs. Above all, he meets face-to-face with managers and workers. In 2003, after he purchased a company in Nagano, he spent three days a week there, touring its factory and meeting with everyone. Over a one-year period he had 25 working dinners with 327 people of the rank of section manager or higher, and 52 working lunches with all 1,056 rank-and-file employees and chiefs. He paid for these get-togethers out of his own pocket, to the tune of 20 million yen. Asked why he takes the time to eat with everyone, he responded this way:

Because when you share a meal and a drink with people, the conversation goes differently. People talk plainly, even when they're just going on about nothing. I take questions. They bring up little things, like they work the day shift but get tired standing on their feet. Or they'll mention that during breaks, there aren't enough chairs, things like that. Why they don't take care of it on the spot I don't know, but anyway people will tell you their opinion. They think their work clothes look like prison uniforms. They wonder why male workers get badges and female workers don't. All sorts of issues emerge, and we solve them all, one after another. That's the purpose of the lunch and dinner meetings.[12]

Notice the similarity between what Nagamori says here and the comments of chef Takeshi Shinmura above ("Face-to-face Management," p. 20). No less than Shinmura, Nagamori is concerned with meeting people face-to-face in order to increase motivation and draw out everyone's full potential, a style of interaction with direct ties to the world of Kyoto craftsmanship. As he is fond of pointing out, "Ability may increase five times, awareness a hundred times."

Nagamori also advocates something he calls a "federated management structure." The idea is that some people, though unsuited to heading a company with a workforce of 100,000, can manage one of 2,000 with no difficulty; fifty such managers can be trained by combining fifty 2,000-man companies into a federation.[13] This approach assumes that companies have an optimum size, an idea frequently discussed in Kyoto. As touched on above, quantitative expansion is difficult in companies using a management system based on values derived from the world of traditional craftsmanship. Optimum size then means the size at which it is possible to manage a company while maintaining face time with the entire workforce.

Amoeba Management

The federated management structure that Nagamori advocates is something that he seeks to implement in his acquisitions. The system is doubtless aimed in part at ensuring company integrity after he retires.

In Kyoto, there is one company that is run entirely by a system similar to the one envisioned by Nagamori. Kyocera Corporation uses the famous "Amoeba management" system, the brainchild of Kazuo Inamori, company founder and chairman emeritus. According to Inamori, the idea grew out of the rapid expansion of his business. With a workforce exceeding three hundred, he remained personally responsible for product development, production, and sales, a situation he realized was untenable. Acutely aware of his limitations and the adverse effect on the business of having a single overseer, he came up with the idea of dividing the company into smaller units of twenty to thirty people, each with a leader of its own. Kyocera consists of minimal business units under separate leadership operated, in his words, "using an independent accounting system, much like small town factories."[14] The choice of words—"small town factories"—is significant. Amoeba Management values close personal interaction and as such is very much in the tradition of Kyoto craftsmanship. Inamori further states that his philosophy of management is "based in the human heart," and that when the thousands of amoeba-like pods comprising the company work together with one accord, the company is truly unified.

Inamori also said, "Even if they are sometimes in competition, the amoebas have to respect and help one another if the company is to display its full potential. This presupposes that all, from the top down to constituent members of amoebas, are bound by bonds of trust."[15] In other words, he believes in face-to-face management and constant improvement in friendly rivalry, the very principles at the heart of Kyoto craft culture.

The Pursuit of Creativity and High Market Share

Kyoto has many creative enterprises that have captured a high share of the global market with unique products. To name just a few, there are Nintendo game consoles such as the Nintendo Switch and Wii, Murata Manufacturing's multilayer ceramic capacitors, Horiba's emission measurement system, Kyocera's applied ceramic-related products and parts, and Rohm's customized semiconductors. The same is true even of relatively new startup firms. Nidec Corporation dominates the market for small precision motors, and Samco has a unique assortment of products, including semiconductor production equipment using thin film deposition.

The uniqueness and high quality of such products enables Kyoto startup firms to win out in competition against much larger firms. Kataoka Corporation, which manufactures laser processing equipment, presents a good example. In the field of inspection systems for the lithium-ion batteries used in electric vehicles, the company has a 50 percent share of the global market, and in the field of ultraprecision laser drilling devices used in the testing of semiconductors and printed circuit boards, it has a 60 percent share. Even though its competitors are much larger, Kataoka has a continually winning record. The company president, Koji Kataoka, made this comment:

Newspaper reporters often ask me, 'Mr. Kataoka, how do you acquire top market share?' I say you can't do it by winning once or twice. You can't be number one without winning consistently. Win once and you might be able to lower your prices and increase orders, but it takes consistency to stay number one while making a profit. Consistent victory is key. Companies like ours with capital of under 500 million yen and a workforce of only 100 lose out if we try to compete against major firms on all fronts. But in a limited field, we have a fighting chance. If we specialized in lasers, wherever we went we'd be up against a big listed company. In Japan, we're the only small business in the field. Fortunately, the market isn't huge. When it comes to fine lasers, or processing with lasers, we can compete. Making it to the top in limited areas such as these is our corporate strategy. Whenever we develop a new product, I ask whoever's in charge, 'Can we be number one with this? Can we be the best in Japan, the best in the world?'[16]

The Art of Differentiation

It goes without saying that the focus on increasing added value by the creation of uniqueness is allied with the nature of Kyoto craftspeople. Samco CEO Osamu Tsuji, who is familiar with the status of Kyoto's high-tech firms, made these comments:

Kyoto firms are aware that they are located in the center of monozukuri, and so they attach importance to having new products, new technologies, and creativity. Nothing is so shameful as imitation, they believe. And so Kyoto firms make products with high added value.

The national model, or the Tokyo model, is to pack up and move to another part of the country when land prices go high. That's common sense, and it doesn't lead to any great progress, does it? Land prices in Kyoto are high. Land in Fushimi ward, where our factory is, runs 900,000 to a million yen per tsubo.[17] *That's exactly why we seek to increase added value. Companies that make semiconductors in a big city, the way Rohm does, are rare anywhere in the world. That makes Rohm quite unique.*

If I were asked what I consider the basis of the management strategy of Kyoto firms to be, I would say it's the emphasis on differentiation. How are we different from others? How are we different from other companies, other prefectures? Kyoto firms have distinguished themselves by creating all sorts of differences, I would say.'[18]

This strategy is in the DNA of Nintendo, the behemoth of the gaming console industry. During his 53-year tenure as president, Hiroshi Yamauchi (1927–2013) elevated the company to its current position by turning it from a local manufacturer of playing cards into a manufacturer of electronic games. He was fond of saying, "We don't do the same things others do." He also made the following statement:

'There already is such-and-such kind of game, and if we just tweak it and improve it maybe we can do business.' Anytime you start thinking like that, things won't go well. That's why our motto at Nintendo is 'we don't make

copies of other companies' products.' I've always made it a point to avoid doing that. That's why I used all my energy in the search for and creation of new patterns.[19]

Satoru Iwata, Yamauchi's successor, said, "Nintendo's strength stems in large part from the thinking of our former president, Hiroshi Yamauchi. The company has been able to retain its strength even during generational change because veteran workers convey his thinking to young colleagues."[20] Iwata went on to warn that unchecked quantitative expansion could threaten Nintendo's position of strength.

Our company is far from big. If we were to increase our workforce tenfold, we'd lose our uniqueness. We're able to remain competitive against large firms precisely because we pare ourselves down to our areas of strength and discard the rest. Becoming a jack-of-all-trades would cost us our individuality and good qualities. Being sharply focused is what enables us to take on giant opponents like Microsoft and Sony.[21]

The business activities of Nintendo set it apart from Kyoto's inner circle of firms, yet its corporate culture and strategy are strongly aligned with Kyoto traditions. This is part of what makes Kyoto business so interesting.

Networks of Kyotoites

There is no doubt that Kyotoites' taste for authenticity lies behind the emphasis on creativity in Kyoto firms. Atsushi Horiba, executive chairman and Group CEO of Horiba, is a man of rich experience who has studied and worked abroad. Past chairman of the Kyoto Association of Corporate Executives, he is a leading figure in the Kyoto business world. Horiba says flatly that the taste for authenticity lies at the heart of Kyoto culture.

The biggest point of Kyoto culture, I believe, is insistence on the genuine article. People here compete on content rather than scale. Choosing quality over quantity comes from their sense of values. At meetings of Kyoto managers, who takes the seat of honor? Whether it's a heritage industry or a modern industry, if a business has remained at the top in its field for a long time, then its representative takes the seat of honor as a matter of course, even if the workforce numbers only twenty or so. A listed company employing thousands with net sales in the billions of yen takes a lower seat if its standing is less than stellar. This is standard in Kyoto.[22]

The ability of Kyotoites to identify what is genuine is closely connected to managers' network of intimates. Horiba offers a glimpse of how the network operates:

> *Not one of Kyoto's listed companies was affected by the bubble economy. That's because we only share genuine information. When you go to Tokyo, conversations start, 'Hey, here's a chance to make some real money.' But in Kyoto, there is a network extending beyond the business world, with a climate that allows the sharing of genuine information only. If I decide while in development that I want to learn production techniques, my friend Yasutaka Murata, CEO of Murata Manufacturing, will offer to show me his plant in Hokuriku. 'But let's go in the winter,' he'll say, 'when the crab is good.' He wants to have a good time while he's at it.*
>
> *If I mention to Yoshikata Tsukamoto, CEO of Wacoal Holdings Corp., that my sales channels are weak, he'll give me some advice. 'That gives you more freedom. We have fixed sales channels, so if a catalog maker or someone comes along, our hands are tied. It's an advantage not to have sales channels.' People don't spread false information.*[23]

Kyoto's fellow top-echelon managers are close, whether they are in the same line of business or not. In addition to formal organizations such as the Kyoto Association of Corporate Executives and the Kyoto Chamber of Commerce and Industry, there are all sorts of informal social groups and tie-ups. In these settings, managers can talk familiarly and share genuine information, as Horiba says, while discussing various aspects of management. This system is similar to the network of Kyoto chefs described by Murata of Kikunoi, and harks back to the core concept of constant improvement in friendly rivalry.

The practical, utilitarian value of such a network is clear, but at the same time, socializing informally is fun. Attendees can talk across work boundaries, feel the personal magnetism of other executives, and so expand their circle. Once you are part of this world, the experience is apparently so educational and enjoyable that you can never leave.

Some people would call this network a sign of Kyoto exclusiveness, and they would be right; but at the same time it is a cultural tradition that makes Kyoto strong. The existence of this rich network of personal connections is one reason why regardless of changes in the environment, Kyoto businesses—unlike firms in neighboring Osaka, for example—insist on keeping their main offices where they are and would never consider moving away.

Such relationships go beyond top-level managers of large firms. Kyoto has the infrastructure to continuously train young, up-and-coming managers, widening the circle yet more. The Kyoto Industrial Association is a good example. With "aiming for a new monozukuri community for the twenty-first century" as its guiding principle, the association trains cutting-edge technicians at the Kyoto High Technology Academy and other educational institutions, as well as providing regular opportunities for fellow executives to interact.

The Egret Club is an organization founded to promote communication among young executives and newly-appointed successors of small and medium-sized enterprises in the Kyoto Industrial Association. The EC has met once a month for the last forty years and counts many company presidents among its alumni. Koji Kataoka, a former member, declares, "The EC made me who I am today." He also says enthusiastically that other executives in the Kyoto Industrial Association are all friendly and congenial, and socializing with them is "fun, really fun," adding, "The Kyoto environment is marvelous. You can learn so much from other executives. I would never leave Kyoto."

In this way, Kyoto provides an unparalleled synergy of people, culture, and technology that gives the city's firms a strong competitive edge. To quote Atsushi Horiba again,

The house I grew up in was in the neighborhood of Kinkakuji Temple. Traditional Japanese houses are rapidly getting torn down, so I hired miya-daiku [carpenters who build and repair traditional architecture such as temples and shrines] to give it a new lease on life. I left the old house in place and had it entirely refurbished to use as a guest house. One time I invited a Mercedes-Benz production engineer to stay there. He had never had a nice word to say about Horiba products and was always harsh in his opinions, but as we were dining in the guest house, he told me, 'It makes me very happy that our company, DaimlerChrysler, can have business relations with a company that has such fine corporate culture as this.' I realized then that rather than praise for one's products, the ultimate joy comes from praise for one's culture, for one's corporate culture. . . .

In Japan, technology transmitted from person to person is important. Simply Westernizing management is problematic, I think. My idea is to appoint different people in each area, technology, and culture, and tie them together through our shared territorial bond. By so doing I want to uphold the strength of the Horiba brand and our technological innovation capability.[24]

Chapter 1 notes

1 Yoshihiro Murata, "Kyoto-teki shoho no susume" [An encouragement of the Kyoto way of business]. Lecture presented at Doshisha Business School, September 29, 2005.

2 Takeshi Shinmura, Remarks made at Kakushin Juku, Doshisha Business School, July 15, 2007.

3 Hirokazu Kato, Remarks made at Kakushin Juku, Doshisha Business School, July 15, 2007.

4 Murata, 2005

5 Ibid.

6 Yunosuke Kawabe, "CG yuzen no kanosei: Atene Gorin to shinkuro mizugi seisaku no butaiura" [Possibilities of CG yuzen: Behind the scenes of making swimwear for the synchronized swimming team at the Athens Olympics]. Lecture presented at Doshisha Business School, May 28, 2005.

7 Akira Shigeyama, "Kyoto=Nippon no kokoro o urimahyo!" [Let's sell the heart of Kyoto=Japan!]. Lecture presented at Doshisha Business School, May 7, 2005.

8 Murata, 2005.

9 Osamu Tsuji, "Kyo yoshiki keiei to monozukuri tetsugaku" [Kyoto-style management and the philosophy of manufacturing]. Lecture presented at Doshisha Business School, September 10, 2005.

10 "Kaisha saiko: baishu eno 'koi' 16 nen kake joju" [Reconsidering companies: A 'love' for acquisition consummated after 16 years]. Asahi Shimbun, August 9, 2007.

11 "Baishu koja: Nagamori shiki no nengajo" [Acquisition expertise: Nagmori-style New Year's cards]. Nihon Keizai Shimbun, January 23, 2018.

12 Nihon Keizai Shimbunsha, ed. Nippon Densan: Nagamori-izumu no chosen [Nidec: Nagamori-ism takes on the world]. Tokyo: Nihon Keizai Shimbunsha, 2004, p. 102-3.

13 Ibid. p. 267.

14 Kazuo Inamori, Ameba keiei [Amoeba management]. Tokyo: Nihon Keizai Shimbunsha, 2006, p. 27-29.

15 Ibid. p. 23.

16 Koji Kataoka, "Nitchi toppu o mezashita keiei senryaku" [Management strategy aimed at reaching the top of a niche market]. Lecture presented at Doshisha Business School, June 25, 2005.

17 A unit of measure equivalent to the area of two tatami mats, roughly 3.3 m^2.

18 Kataoka, 2005.

19 Kenji Takahashi, Nintendo shoho no himitsu [Secrets of Nintendo business]. Tokyo: Shodensha, 1986, p. 173.

20 "Iwata-san ni kiku" [Asking Iwata Satoru]. Asahi Shimbun, January 4, 2008.

21 Nintendo wa naze tsuyoi? [Why is Nintendo strong?] Nikkei Business. December 17, 2007, p. 31.

22 Atsushi Horiba, "Kyoto bunka to gurobaru tenkai" [Kyoto culture and global development] at Doshisha Business School, July 23, 2005.

23 Ibid.

24 Ibid.

Chapter 2

•

Combining Tradition and Technology

KYOTO'S STRENGTH AS A CITY LIES IN THE COEXISTENCE OF HERITAGE AND HIGH-tech industries. The previous chapter examined how management of both types of firm embraces elements of craftsmanship. Here, concrete examples of relations between heritage and high-tech industries will be introduced, showing their mutual influence.

1. The Influence of Heritage Industries on High-tech Industries

The Ceramic Industry and Murata Manufacturing

Looking at the history of business in Kyoto, it is evident that heritage industries have given rise to many of the city's high-tech industries. A classic example is the relationship between ceramics and Murata Manufacturing, which currently holds about 40 percent of the global market for multilayer ceramic capacitors. The company makes parts for a wide range of the electronic goods that underpin our digital society, including smartphones, laptop computers, and flat-screen TVs. As it happens, the origins of this innovative company are inseparably tied to the tradition of ceramics in Kyoto.

The father of company founder Akira Murata was born in Ishikawa Prefecture and, after being orphaned at an early age, went to Kyoto to be apprenticed to a kimono merchant. Later, in part because his younger sister and her husband ran a ceramics store in Kyoto, Murata's father sold the family rice fields in Ishikawa to raise the capital necessary to establish a company. Initially, the business he established focused on ceramic insulators for use in shipboard light sockets and the like. From around the turn of the century, in addition to the domestic and overseas markets for traditional ceramic wares, insulators were being made for export as a means of revitalizing and diversifying the local ceramics industry. The leader in the manufacture of ceramic insulators was then Shofu Industries, founded in Kyoto in 1906. Amid this changing scene, Murata's father started an insulator factory in the compound of Sennyuji Temple in Higashiyama, the hub of Kyoto's ceramics industry.

Akira (1921–2006) assisted in the family business by doing bookkeeping and calling on customers, but he was unsatisfied and wanted to expand by seeking out new customers. His plan, however, met with resistance. His father explained that accepting new orders would entail stealing customers from others in the same line of business by charging lower prices, a breach of professional etiquette. Accordingly, Akira resolved to branch out in an entirely new direction and develop a unique product that would not infringe on anyone else's territory. Producing independently developed, unique products remains basic policy at Murata Manufacturing to this day, further evidence of the Kyoto penchant for originality.

Then Akira encountered a book called *Specialized Ceramic Products* that indicated to him the potential for developing new ceramics utilizing chemical properties. He had little practical knowledge of such applications, however, and knew that studying just on his own would not be enough. Accordingly, he turned for guidance to the National Ceramics Laboratory that was then in Kyoto. It had started life in 1896 as the Kyoto Municipal Ceramics Laboratory, established jointly by the city of Kyoto and a ceramics trade association. The goal was to seek improvement and progress through research and education, with special emphasis on researching the chemical elements of ceramics. Akira fortunately was able to acquire an abundance of technological expertise.

In this way, Akira Murata was able to begin developing and producing specialized ceramics. Soon he was producing insulators used in airplanes as well as the ceramic capacitors that are Murata's main products today, thus laying the foundation for the company's development after World War II. Murata Manufacturing took advantage of the postwar boom in electric appliances as well as subsequent computerization. The company maintained high growth, ultimately capturing the top position it holds today.

The Link between Kyocera and Ceramic Insulation

As described above, the infrastructure of the traditional ceramics industry in Kyoto played a large role in the establishment and development of Murata Manufacturing. A similar fascinating link also exists between the same industry and Kyocera, founded in 1959 by Kazuo Inamori.

Born in Kagoshima Prefecture down in Kyushu, Inamori attended Kagoshima University and before graduation sought a job in the field of petrochemistry. However, despite applying to a great many companies, he had no success. He consulted with his university professor, who informed him that he knew someone in Kyoto who was involved in the manufacture of ceramic insulators. Thus began Inamori's connection with the city. He went to work at Shofu Industries and was assigned to study new ceramic materials, especially forsterite, a high-frequency insulator. He became immersed in his work and succeeded in making a ceramic insulation component for the electron gun of a cathode-ray TV tube, which had been custom ordered by Matsushita Electronics Industry Corporation (now Panasonic). However, by then Shofu Industries was in decline, and company morale was low. Eager to move on, Inamori took several colleagues with him and founded his own company, Kyoto Ceramic—the forerunner of Kyocera.

The story of Kyocera's origins is strikingly similar to the birth of semiconductor startup firms in Silicon Valley. However, what lies behind the birth of both Murata Manufacturing and Kyocera is ceramic insulation and the traditional world of Kyoto ceramics. Here we see a path of development unique to Kyoto: a heritage industry giving rise to a high-tech company, which in turn gives rise to a startup.

Horiba's High-Mix, Low-Volume Production Challenge

The pattern of heritage industries evolving into high-tech industries exists to this day in Kyoto.

Toshihiko Uno, Horiba's auditor, was formerly the company's general manager of production and executive officer. When he was in charge of production, Uno spearheaded the shift to computerization. At the time, Horiba, which implements classic high-mix, low-volume production, manufactured over 1,300 products. The lot sizes for printed circuit board (PCB) production were generally fewer than twenty per product line, and sometimes there was a single circuit board per job lot. That hampered computerization. Thus Uno, with his extensive experience with digital technology, was handed the challenging task of automating the company's production processes.

Uno was born the son of a kimono maker in the Muromachi neighborhood of Kyoto, but instead of following in the family business he chose to pursue a career in the unrelated but fascinating field of technology. He was fortunate in landing a job at the legendary firm of Busicom, designer of the world's first microprocessor, which Intel eventually marketed as the Intel 4004, the first commercially available microprocessor. Uno's job at this highly innovative and technologically advanced firm was the design of computing machines. Following a stint at the British branch of Busicom, he went to work for Horiba at the invitation of founder Masao Horiba. First, he set about digitalizing Horiba products in development, which were then mainly analog. Next he was put in charge of production.

In order to digitalize the Horiba factory, he had to begin by digitalizing circuit board production, but all did not go well. The bottleneck turned out to be the method of soldering used when surface mounting integrated circuit chips on a PCB. At that time, solder was dropped through open holes in a screen. That technique was suitable for large-scale production where the same pattern was soldered over and over; however, given Horiba's high-mix, low-volume production, it was inefficient and costly, necessitating a new screen for every change of pattern.

Utilizing a Traditional Technique

To solve the problem, Uno turned to a traditional technique of applying gold powder to fabric that he remembered from his family's kimono-making business. The technique had been imported from China during the Heian period (794–1185), but fell out of use in the Edo period (1603–1868) due to sumptuary laws that caused common people to stop spending money on expensive kimonos. By the mid nineteenth century, the technique had virtually disappeared, but Kyoto craftspeople revived it during the Meiji period (1868–1912). They mixed gold powder and rice paste in a tube, squeezing it to draw delicate lines on the cloth. The technique is strongly identified with the style of Kyoto *yuzen* kimono.

Uno asked himself whether it might not be possible to apply solder to a PCB in the same way that craftspeople apply gold paste to a kimono design. Based on his idea, with the help of Hitachi Techno Engineering, the "maskless printer" came into being. Uno connected a computer containing design information with the PCB production center so that, using computer-aided design input, solder could be "drawn" on circuit boards. In short, he developed a high-tech system by employing techniques used in making hand-painted *yuzen* kimono.

Using such techniques, Uno was able to deliver an automated system that would work even for a single PCB. Along with contracting the design-to-production timeline by nearly two thirds, the new system saves tens of millions of yen annually. This account affords a glimpse of the magnificent way in which the human element, traditional culture, and technology combine in a way representative of Kyoto. Such a combination has given Horiba a strong competitive edge.

2. The Influence of High-Tech Industries on Heritage Industries

Mechanization of Manual Labor

Next, let us examine what influence there may have been in the other direction. What impact has the high-tech world had on heritage industries? Here the connection is not as evident. That is because mechanizing traditional manual labor would not necessarily revitalize heritage industries. Of course, the process itself would lower costs and increase productivity. But as already mentioned, losing work done by hand would result in products losing their distinctive flavor and the added value of their culture. As this chapter will show, it is still possible to mechanize heritage industries in part, while leaving critical handmade processes intact, but in any case, combining craftspeople's handiwork with mechanization is extremely hard to do, and therein lies the unique problem of the world of craftsmanship.

American-Style Solution

Looking back in history, most industries were entirely hand-operated in the beginning. They became more efficient through the introduction of technology, allowing them to develop further. The automotive industry is a classic example. In Europe, where the automobile originated, at the end of the nineteenth century automobiles were made by skilled craftspeople. Manufacturers consigned the production of automotive parts to factories scattered around town, which achieved "hand-fitted craftsmanship in which the gaps between individual parts were nearly invisible."[1] As a result, no two finished automobiles were exactly alike, and they cost so much that only the very wealthy could afford one.

This customized production of automobiles went through a revolutionary change in the United States, brought about by the famous Model T Ford. Henry Ford introduced his well-known belt conveyor system of mass production that made possible the automation of automobile manufacturing. He changed the production of automobiles from a system where all parts were handmade to one where parts were subdivided, standardized, and made interchangeable. That in turn made it possible for assembly to be done by unskilled labor. Finished products became standardized and indistinguishable from one another. The Model T Ford came in one design and one color only—black.

This system lowered labor costs and spurred further rationalization, greatly increasing the efficiency of production and reducing the time needed for assembly by nearly 90 percent. Prices plummeted. The price of a Model T rolling off the assembly line went down by more than 40 percent. Affordable prices led to a surge in demand that brought huge profits, making Henry Ford a multimillionaire.

The Dilemma of Mechanizing Heritage Industries

The example of the Model T shows clearly what happens when production of hand-built items is standardized. This is the classic American-style solution to the problem of inefficient manual labor: streamline production using technology, thereby lowering costs and expanding the market. Can this solution be applied to the heritage industries of Kyoto, which rely heavily on labor-intensive hand crafting? Doing so would certainly solve the problem of high costs, which would in turn expand the market. However, the triple threat this approach would inflict upon heritage industries cannot be ignored.

First, as has been repeatedly stressed, imposing uniformity deprives products of the subtle charm of craftsmanship. Uniformity being a primary goal of industrialization, that appeal unfortunately would have to be sacrificed, which poses a risk of imperiling the heritage industries.

The second threat is also serious. Namely, anyone who acquires the necessary hardware can copy the products. This is not of course an unmitigated evil, as in the normal course of things, imitation spurs competition, leading to lower costs and increased efficiency. In the case of Kyoto's heritage industries, however, if imitations were to flood the market, a price war might ensue, making it harder to attach added cultural value. Such a development would doom heritage industries.

Third is the danger to morale. Craftspeople are confident in the workmanship of their products, which depend on manual labor, and antagonistic to the idea of changing methods they have used all their lives. To introduce technology in the workplace and change production even in part could well shake their faith in the meaning of their work.

All three threats are part of what we may call "the dilemma of mechanizing heritage industries." Mechanization can reduce costs and stir demand, but it can also destroy the cultural value of heritage industries and cause them to lose significance. Yet if those industries continue to rely solely on manual labor, productivity won't rise and personnel costs will put pressure on earnings. What are some ways to meet this dilemma head on? In the sections below, we will consider Fukujuen's successful development of Iyemon tea for packaging in PET bottles and Yunosuke Kawabe's experiment with CG *yuzen*, two fascinating examples of how technology can open new possibilities for heritage industries.

Introducing Traditional Techniques into Technology

As president of Fukujuen, a leading firm in the heritage industry of green tea manufacturing, Masanori Fukui actively promoted research and development as well as process mechanization and automation. At the instigation of the government, simple machinery was introduced for the final drying of tea leaves, a process known as *hiire* (firing), but Fukui called into question its suitability. Born into a family that has been manufacturing tea for generations, he recalled hearing even as a young child that *hiire* involves the kneading of the leaves. However, the drying machines were designed simply to remove moisture, without consideration of *neri* (kneading), a traditional step that ensures maximum flavor and aroma. Accordingly, he found a way to mechanize *neri* and include it in the drying process.

In Fukui's words, "tradition contains the human aspect of technology," and "humanity and technology cannot be compartmentalized." While continuing to support the mechanization of tea manufacture, he places full value on the traditional, human aspects of tea-making.

The Secret of Iyemon's Flavor

Fukui's stance is evident in the making and marketing of Iyemon tea, a hugely popular brand of ready-to-drink tea. He assesses the tea's success as follows:

> Some say it's the name 'Iyemon,' others say it's Rie Miyazawa [the actress who appears in commercials for the tea], but actually content is the critical factor behind the success of the drink. Iyemon is recognized in the beverage industry as a whole, and also in the tea industry, as a drink with authentic flavor. We at Fukujuen have the knowhow to make authentic tea, and Suntory

has gone to great lengths to provide fine water for its wines and whiskies. Those two technologies came together perfectly.[2]

Fukui credits the success of Iyemon tea in large part to the technological prowess of the two companies involved in its development. In deciding whom to partner with, he took into account Suntory's expertise in nonthermal aseptic filling and water-related technology, especially extraction. Bottled tea made using the former technology, instead of sterilizing by heating as before, preserves the tea's full flavor. Sterilizing by heating would amount to reheating the brewed tea, which of course would harm the flavor. Because Suntory possessed the needed technology for nonthermal aseptic filling and had a strong record in extracting water for beverage products, Fukujuen was able to take on the challenge of developing tea for PET bottles that "tastes as good as if it came from a teapot."

Fukujuen's expertise in the art of blending tea proved equally invaluable. The needed ingredients for leaf tea and bottled tea naturally differ, as do the methods of blending. In addition to flavor, the color and shape of tea leaves is significant for leaf tea, but not for bottled tea. Although the criteria for choosing tea leaves may differ, the fundamental blending technology is the same. In the past, blends for bottled tea were made somewhat the way a pharmacist concocts medicine, by adding and subtracting various leaf types to enhance or diminish flavor as needed. Fukujuen took a different approach, deciding to use a blend suitable for teapot brewing. Rather than adding and subtracting flavors the old-fashioned way, researchers focused on the flavor synergy generated by leaf combinations, drawing on years of tea-making knowhow to achieve the desired taste profile. Fukujuen's inimitable blending technology was utilized to the full in making Iyemon tea.

Fukujuen was able to make good use of its expertise in part because it collaborated with Suntory as an equal partner rather than as a subordinate. Fukujuen's ideas were implemented in the blending, and that, combined with Suntory's expertise in nonthermal aseptic filling and extraction, led to the creation of the rich Iyemon flavor.

Fukui declares himself happy with the flavor of Iyemon tea. Indeed, if he had not been fully satisfied with the product, he would hardly have allowed it to bear the name of his ancestor, the man who founded Fukujuen over two centuries ago. The combination of Fukujuen's traditional knowhow and

Photo 6: Yuzen lanterns ∂esigne∂ by Yunosuke Kawabe. Digital technology ma∂e it possible to ∂ecorate streets with the beauty of kimono.

Photo: Yunosuke Kawabe

Suntory's advanced technology led to the creation of a bottled green-tea product on which the centuries-old family enterprise was proud to bestow its name.

The Work of Yunosuke Kawabe

I have already described how Yunosuke Kawabe, who was born into a family of *yuzen* dyers, is opening a new chapter in the history of Kyoto *yuzen* through CG *yuzen*, a new field that combines this heritage industry with modern technology.

Although the son of a *yuzen* dyer, Kawabe entered the field of graphic design after being struck by a poster for the Montreal Olympics. After graduating from vocational school, he went to work for an advertising company, but then left to return home and help out with the family business. Having glimpsed the glittery wider world, however, he found the conventional world of *yuzen* dyeing stifling and unfulfilling. Through a repeated process of trial and error, he came up with the idea of integrating traditional *yuzen*

Photo 7: Kawabe ∂esigne∂ these striking swimsuits for the Japanese swimming team at the 2004 Athens Olympics, using tra∂itional color schemes an∂ ∂esigns.

Photo: Yunosuke Kawabe

designs with the latest computer technology, which was just then taking off. By breaking down the *yuzen* manufacturing process and reconstructing it on the computer, he came up with something brand-new: CG *yuzen*.

Kawabe has continued to explore new possibilities for CG *yuzen* in areas from swimwear to interior decoration. For New Year's Eve in 2000, to mark the start of the new millennium he used CG *yuzen* technology to create colorful 3-meter-tall standing lanterns that lit up the night. *(See photo 6, above left.)* Revelers walking down Oike Street in Kyoto enjoyed the magical ambience created by the glowing lanterns. The swimwear worn by Japanese synchronized swimmers in the 2004 Athens Olympics are some of his representative work, along with T-shirts worn by former Yankee outfielder Hideki Matsui and the baseball jacket favored by former Chunichi Dragons manager Hiromitsu Ochiai. *(See photo 7, above.)* Kawabe is extending the concept of integrating *yuzen* into modern daily life, using CG *yuzen* in everything from tote bags and other small articles to sofas, chairs, and cushions, not to mention watches, bookbinding, and even greeting cards.

Computer Graphics *Yuzen* and Authentic *Yuzen*

It is important to note that Kawabe is not merely taking traditional *yuzen* designs and transferring them to other media via CG. He himself has mastered the various techniques of traditional hand-painted *yuzen* and incorporates them into CG *yuzen*. One important consideration is color distribution. Styles differ among the different *yuzen* workshops, each of which each has its own ways of creating rich color effects through particular color combinations, intensities, and so on. Such characteristics provide the subtle nuances that give *yuzen* dyeing its distinctive, pleasing aesthetic. Each workshop's style is unique and inimitable. Kawabe's creations express the tacit knowledge shared in his family, not by brush, as in the past, but by the new tools of computers and CG. His works embody the authentic, living tradition of *yuzen*, which is why the careful observer will note ineradicable similarities between his works and the hand-painted *yuzen* kimono lovingly crafted by his father Zenji. By combining the core of centuries-old tradition with his own keen sensibility and modern CG technology, Kawabe has carved out a new product category where business innovation and technology go hand-in-hand with tradition.

Overcoming Dilemmas

Fukujuen's Iyemon tea and Yunosuke Kawabe's CG *yuzen* each transformed a heritage industry so that mechanization and mass production became possible. At the same time, those two products have gone a long way toward solving the dilemmas inherent in the process of modernization. Fukujuen met the first dilemma, the loss of handcrafted value, by bringing craftsmanship to bear in tea contained in PET bottles, with the aid of Suntory technology. With CG *yuzen*, since Kawabe is himself a *yuzen* artist fully trained in the ancient craft, he draws on traditional craftsmanship in the work he does on computer.

Bringing traditional knowhow to bear in the technology used to create these new products also lowers the risk of indiscriminate copying, the second dilemma. Even with the identical equipment, no one could possibly reproduce the distinctive flavor of Iyemon tea, as it depends on Fukujuen's secret blend of tea leaves. Someone knowledgeable in CG might be able to copy Kawabe's designs to an extent, but careful examination will always show a marked difference between his creations and those of imitators.

Then what of the third threat, negative impact on worker morale? Masanori Fukui freely admits that as president of a company famous for leaf tea he felt some resistance about putting out a beverage in PET bottles for mass consumption. He talked himself into it by reasoning that the world's top makers of brand goods offer a range of items from formal to casual, so why not make a bottled tea that would be the best among ready-to-drink beverages? Once his mind was made up, the craftsman in him grew excited, and when development work for Iyemon tea was finished, he told me, "For the first time in quite a while, I felt a strong sense of accomplishment in manufacturing tea."

Yunosuke Kawabe's case is similar. While he felt a slight pang at leaving the family business, he put that behind him and now feels highly motivated, having launched *yuzen* through the new medium of CG. Recent years have seen him greatly expand the scope of his creative activities.

The Frontier of Japanese Technology

The stories of Masanori Fukui and Yunosuke Kawabe each illustrate a distinctive use of technology aptly summed up in Fukui's idea that tradition contains the human aspect of technology. Effective use of new technology in heritage industries must include the human element. Incorporating the craftsman's spirit in technological innovations offers a solution to the inherent challenges involved in mechanizing heritage industries and suggests the hidden potential of welding technology to traditional craftsmanship.

The sort of transfer between heritage industries and high-tech industries seen in the examples of Murata Manufacturing, Kyocera, and Horiba shows a fine interplay among people, technology, and tradition or culture. This tendency deep in Kyoto's heart or built into its DNA gives high-tech businesses their competitive edge and opens new possibilities for heritage industries as well.

In that sense, the combination of tradition and technology is a field of great latent potential not only for Kyoto but for the Japanese economy as a whole. Japanese big businesses are beginning to take note of the techniques used in Kyoto's heritage industries, and new collaborations are being formed. This trend is highly significant for the future of the nation's economy, a topic explored further in Chapter 7.

Chapter 2 notes

1. James P. Womack, Daniel T. Jones, and Daniel Roos, *The Machine that Changed the World: The Story of Lean Production*. New York: Rawson Associates, 1990, p. 23.

2. Masanori Fukui. "Chikyu ni zokushiteiru Nihon, Kyoto, soshite wagasha" [They all belong to the Earth: Japan, Kyoto, and our company]. Lecture presented at Doshisha Business School, June 18, 2005.

Chapter 3

•

*Creating New Value
from Cultural Capital*

IN THINKING OF KYOTO, HOW TO APPROACH THE CITY'S HISTORICAL ASSETS FROM a business perspective is of enormous importance. This chapter will focus on continuity, a major characteristic of businesses related to Kyoto culture, and the challenge of generating new business from the city's cultural capital. The key point to remember is that culture and business both operate in tandem with society and people.

1. Culture Supported by the Common People

Long-Established Family Enterprises That Thrive

Kyoto is rare in the world for the number of centuries-old family enterprises it boasts. The tea company Fukujuen was founded 229 years ago. Of the businesses taken up in this chapter, the incense shop Shoyeido was founded over three hundred years ago, and the venerable restaurant Hyotei dates back nearly four centuries. The lineage of the Shigeyama family, masters of kyogen, extends back some thirteen generations.

Over the course of its 1,200-year history, Kyoto has been the scene of numerous power struggles, and the ruling class has experienced great vicissitudes. While the upper class has had the authority to support Kyoto culture, that support was not always forthcoming. After 1869, when the national capital shifted east to Tokyo, courtiers who had served as patrons of Kyoto's cultural businesses were suddenly nowhere to be found. Still, the old family businesses of Kyoto overcame such shocks and managed to thrive.

Kyotoites Are *Komakai*

To remain in business in Kyoto, where patronage and support could be cut off at any time, required great resilience. Many Kyoto merchants are what is called *komakai*—a Japanese word that can mean someone who is a stickler for details, but when applied to Kyotoites means "close-fisted" or, more bluntly, "stingy."

In the Nishijin district of Kyoto where I grew up, there was a candy store where as a boy I used to go every day. I became friends with the old couple who ran the store, and they took quite a shine to me. Not once in all the times I went there, however, did they ever give me a discount on a purchase. Sometimes the owner would give me an interesting piece of driftwood or some such thing, but neither he nor his wife ever slipped me anything for free or for a lower price. Looking back, I can see that their approach was wise, a way of protecting their livelihood. They treated kids like me as regular customers, and the profits they made from our business helped them keep going. No matter how fond of one of us they might be, that never translated into a lower price. That attitude is typical not just of candy store owners but of Kyoto merchants in general.

That hardheaded approach to business, which some might regard as cold, appears somehow at odds with the brilliance of Kyoto culture and the slow tempo of life in the old capital. To outsiders, it makes Kyotoites seem strange. But to ensure the continuance of any heritage industry, where business and culture are intertwined, this close-fisted approach is a must. Kyoto shopkeepers are unrelentingly careful where money is concerned so that they can remain self-reliant.

Western Theatrical Arts, Chronically in the Red

To better understand the characteristics of business and culture in Kyoto, I'd like to examine some differences between Kyoto and the West in the state of the performing arts, which bear many similarities to heritage industries. I'll begin by summarizing a classic study of culture and economy that deals with the performing arts. The authors' conclusion is not limited to the performing arts but applies equally to the work of craftspeople.

American economists William J. Baumol and William G. Bowen analyzed the economic condition of the performing arts in a 1966 book called *Performing Arts: The Economic Dilemma*. They concluded that live theatrical arts will always operate in the red. Performing arts cannot benefit from the sort of technological innovation seen in manufacturing, while personnel costs, which account for the greatest proportion of expenses, can only rise, dragged along by the general increase in labor costs. Therefore, the cost of live performances can only go up.

Baumol and Bowen noted the impracticality of coping with rising costs by increasing ticket prices, the major source of income for the performing arts. Aside from ethical concerns about jacking up ticket prices, competition from other forms of entertainment is sure to cause the boomerang effect of decreased attendance. They concluded, based on empirical studies, that the income gaps of performing organizations are inevitable: the performing arts are, by their very nature, prone to operating in the red.

They also argued that because the performing arts are beneficial to society, beyond the interests of those directly involved in their production, and because their enjoyment must not be restricted unfairly to the wealthy, governmental support for them is worthy of consideration.

Countries around the world responded to this call for action by establishing public funds to support the performing arts and by forming societies such as the Association for Cultural Economics International to advance research in the economic aspects of the arts and cultural sector. In addition to shaping research trends in cultural economics and cultural policy, Baumol and Bowen's seminal study has had enormous impact on actual cultural policies.

Kyogen, an Art of the People

Notwithstanding the rigor of Baumol and Bowen's analysis, cultural economics established in the West are not applicable to the cultural businesses of Kyoto, whose existence is predicated on staying out of the red. This is certainly true of traditional theatrical arts, and for many years now great efforts have been made to ensure that Kyoto's live performing arts remain economically viable. To illustrate this, let's return to the Shigeyama family.

Akira Shigeyama, born in 1952, calls kyogen "the Yoshimoto Shinkigeki[1] of the Muromachi period" (1333–1573). Originally the performing art of peasants and townsmen, kyogen was also the vernacular entertainment of its day. This is why it not only includes nonsense, jokes, and antiestablishment satire, but also incorporates elements of the erotic and even of the grotesque. Later, he says, as it came under the patronage of the Tokugawa, it gradually evolved into a more refined and polished form of comedy. To restore kyogen to its former status as an art of the everyday, he has performed *ensho* kyogen, "bawdy kyogen," and to restore its contemporaneity he has even branched out into something he calls "SF kyogen." He also helped found the NOHO Theater Group in Kyoto with the goal of fusing theater techniques of Noh and kyogen with Western plays.

Such creativity and experimentalism are a tradition in the Shigeyama family. Sennojo, Akira's father, used to say that the family had a tradition of "not kowtowing to authority." Sennojo's grandfather liked to say "Kyogen is tofu." In the early twentieth century, kyogen was highly formal, but the old patriarch did not like that approach and would perform anywhere he was invited to do so. That sort of kyogen, performed alongside the common people, is what he meant by "tofu." Unlike kyogen in Tokyo, kyogen in the Kyoto-Osaka region has always existed for the common people. The old master's concept of "tofu kyogen" has been continued and further developed by subsequent Shigeyama generations.

Sennojo's Resolve

Sennojo Shigeyama sought by various means to make kyogen an everyday affair. He broke a longstanding taboo in the Noh-kyogen world by performing with kabuki and *shingeki* ("new theater") actors, and even did radio dramas and opera in kyogen style. These actions came under fire from the conservative Nohgaku Performers' Association.

Things came to a head in 1958, when Sennojo was scheduled to appear in a kabuki performance. For a kyogen actor to perform alone in kabuki was unheard of, and people who had supported his other innovations shook their heads at this and advised him to think better of the idea. Particular concern was expressed over potential damage to relations with the Nohgaku Performers' Association. When the association learned from an article in the newspaper what was going on, they sent an official letter of protest. Seeing what an uproar his son's action would cause, his father advised him to abandon the idea, but Sennojo was resolute. He wrote the association a long letter in which he pointed out that nothing in their articles of incorporation imposed any limits on members' artistic performances, and he further threatened that if they objected to his appearance in the kabuki play, he was prepared to resign. He went ahead with the performance and earned glowing reviews. The experiment was a success and the association never took any action.

Sennojo was motivated to take on a new challenge even at the risk of irreparably damaging his career because he was convinced that Noh and kyogen actors should be able to perform as freely as actors in other genres. With a strong sense of mission, he made performing kyogen as contemporary Japanese theater his lifework.

Making Kyogen an Everyday Affair

According to Sennojo, it is the business of kyogen performers to pass on tradition while at the same time creating contemporary kyogen day by day in front of an audience. To that end, the introduction of "school kyogen" in the postwar era had a profound effect. The program was a sort of delivery service to schools, aiming to familiarize children with kyogen early on in their lives. The performances were made part of the curriculum and shown at the schools' request. The program was a resounding success. In May and June in the spring, and in October and November in the fall, the Shigeyama family would make the rounds of schools nearly every day. The schedule was brutal, sometimes calling for five performances in a day; in a span of forty years, Sennojo estimated he performed at "hundreds, no, thousands" of schools. In the immediate postwar period they sometimes were not paid for their performances, but they were glad just to receive a bowl of rice.

"School kyogen" had an incalculable effect on the flourishing of the art. People who saw kyogen when they were children continued to feel an affinity for it when they were grown up and went to see performances. Akira identifies support from that generation as one of the foundations underlying the current kyogen boom. Also, young kyogen actors began taking lead roles in TV dramas. Fans of their TV performances then turned out for kyogen, eager to see their favorite actors live. Not all of those fans will become regular patrons, but some will take an interest in kyogen for its own sake. Television thus offers a wide entryway to the world of kyogen and has been responsible for a bump in attendance.

Citizens' Kyogen Association

Traditional performing arts permeate the air in Kyoto. They have survived in partnership with local people, generation after generation. Kyogen in particular has survived precisely because of efforts to maintain that partnership. One aspect of those efforts can be seen in the Citizens' Kyogen Association of Kyoto, which dates from 1957. In 2005 the association celebrated its two hundredth performance.

In the family of poet Ryoko Hirano, kyogen appreciation through the Citizens' Kyogen Association spans four generations. Hirano still remembers her mother's and grandmother's reactions after the association's first performance in Maruyama Park Bandstand; her grandmother said it was "lively and fun," and her mother said the actors were handsome. She herself has come to appreciate kyogen with a poet's sensibility: "Kyogen isn't just for laughs. It's contemporary theater that explores in words the essence of what it means to be human."[2] Her daughter and her daughter's friends also like to see performances at the Kyoto Kanze Nohplay Theater.

Within the Shigeyama family, as years go by the baton passes to the next generation, and now Akira's son Doji is actively promoting kyogen in his own way. Through changing times, kyogen actors seek always to be part of people's lives, and the people of Kyoto respond with unstinting support. The actors' efforts are rich with suggestion for the preservation of culture over the long haul.

Ryotei and the Townspeople

The wisdom of sustaining business through support from townspeople is found in Kyoto restaurants as well. Chef Yoshihiro Murata of Kikunoi puts it this way:

> *Times are hard for restaurants now. After the bursting of the economic bubble, restaurants in Tokyo and Osaka closed their doors, but not in Kyoto. Hardly any restaurants here did. What kept them from failing? I think it's because people in Kyoto have seen so much change, historically speaking. Once, it was the age of Toyotomi Hideyoshi, and then just like that it was the age of the Tokugawa. People in Kyoto have seen change like that happen over and over. If they did business only with the elite, they'd all be long gone. Restaurants don't exist for the powers that be, but for the common folk. Kyoto restaurant owners know that whatever winds of change may blow, people's lives remain fundamentally the same. That's how Kyoto restaurants have managed to stay in business so long.*
>
> *In this city, people come to a fine restaurant for the first time as newborns, just after their first visit to a shrine for a blessing, held in their grandmother's arms. When it's time for them to get married, they come to meet their prospective spouse or to exchange betrothal gifts. In old age they come to celebrate landmark birthdays, the seventy-seventh or eighty-eighth, and after they die, a get-together in a fine restaurant marks the end of the period of mourning.*
>
> *The way to get people to keep coming at these important junctures in life is to keep prices in a reasonable range. Take the example of a Buddhist memorial service. Attendees bring an envelope containing ten thousand yen, as a rule. Ideally you want them to think, 'I only gave ten thousand yen, but they had the dinner in a fine place like that. I wonder if I gave enough?' What you don't want is for people to think, 'I gave ten thousand yen, but it looks to me like*

they made a fat profit.' Whatever money is received should go toward food and drink—that's the right price. At Kikunoi, we charge eight thousand yen per person. The remaining two or three thousand yen goes for reciprocal funeral presents to attendees. People should think, 'My, they certainly held the service at a nice place, and there was lots of good food.' Create this impression, and your restaurant will fill with customers, at least at lunchtime. We're surrounded by temples too.

Kyoto restaurants set out to be with the people, and that's why at the height of the economic bubble, even when restaurants in Tokyo and Osaka hiked their prices, in Kyoto we absolutely did not.[3]

In Tokyo, the word *ryotei*, denoting a fine Japanese-style restaurant, suggests someplace rather unapproachable. Most people feel that they don't belong in such a place. Kyoto *ryotei* are different; they are an integral part of people's lives. The Nishijin district where I grew up has a number of *ryotei*, and my parents often took me to them for memorial services and on other occasions. They were places where relatives would gather to talk while they ate; as a child, I never thought they were anything special. Now when I visit them as an adult, I see what I missed in childhood: the distinctive Kyoto atmosphere, with beautiful gardens and rooms decorated just so for the season. The function of the *ryotei* is another sign of the way in which Kyoto culture survives because it is rooted in people's lives.

2. Contemporary Value from Historical Assets

The Secret of the Neighborhood Shrine

In the Nishijin district, there is a shrine that the locals refer to as Seimei-san. When I was born, the shrine gave me my name. Seimei-san is located about a fifteen-minute walk from my house, and my grandfather often used to visit it. At the end of the year he would buy a calendar there and show it to me. It contained mysterious alignments of Chinese characters having to do with fortune-telling, and I would gaze at it curiously, wondering what might lie in store for me in the coming year. *(See photo 8, opposite.)*

Not until recently did I learn the significance of the shrine's name. "Seimei" refers to Abe no Seimei (921–1005), a renowned *onmyoji* (divination master). Nowadays he figures prominently in manga, books, movies, and on television, the center of a "Seimei boom" that has brought sightseers flocking to the shrine. At the 2018 Pyeongchang Winter Olympics, figure skater Yuzuru Hanyu's brilliantly executed free program was inspired by Abe no Seimei. Until the Seimei boom, since I knew that the shrine priests had named me, I always thought that the shrine's name meant "first and last name," which is also pronounced *seimei* in Japanese.

The Lessons of Seimei Shrine

When I was a child, the shrine we called Seimei-san was tiny and nondescript, too small to offer a playground. I often did play in other shrine and temple compounds, but I have no memory of ever playing there. Today, however, the surge of interest in Abe no Seimei has made the shrine grounds a popular sightseeing spot with many young visitors. The grounds have been refurbished, and there's even a souvenir shop. In the past this would have been unthinkable.

What ignited the boom was the way novelist Baku Yumemakura and manga artist Reiko Okano created a fresh, contemporary image of Abe no Seimei

Photo 8: Seimei Shrine, which has become a tourist spot in the Nishijin district. On the torii gate is a five-pointed star that symbolizes the shrine's connection to ancient divination. Photo: Yunosuke Kawabe

through their works. Yumemakura says that the very lack of material concerning Seimei's early years freed him to construct his own image of the man. His works portray Seimei, who was said to be versed in astrology and physiognomy and able to perform magic using incantations, as a "beautiful youth, tall, fair of skin and clear of eye." Reborn as a contemporary hero able to fight demons and evil spirits, Seimei became hugely popular among young people especially.

There is much to learn from the reinvention of Abe no Seimei and its effect on the fortunes of Seimei Shrine. For one thing, it shows the importance of reexamining the present day in the light of history. Yumemakura made a thorough study of Abe no Seimei and his era based on available historical documents, and then extracted from that material the elements that would most resonate today, creating a character with contemporary relevance. He then made up stories based on that character.

Kyoto is fortunate to have a long history of rich culture in the first place. Such cultural capital can be mined for new value. The key is to do thorough historical research, analyzing the factors that shaped that history and sifting out what is useful today from what is not. Through this process it is possible to create something new and contemporary, leaving the cultural core untouched, and so generate income from cultural capital. In the case of Seimei Shrine, it wasn't the shrine itself that did the work leading to the shrine's rejuvenation, but two people from outside Kyoto, a novelist and a manga artist.

Of course, people in Kyoto are also engaged in the same sort of work, as the next section will show.

Incense for Our Time

In 1989, Shoyeido Incense, a family enterprise dating back over three hundred years, opened a modern new branch in Kyoto called Lisn, pronounced like the English word "listen." (In the Japanese language, focusing quietly on the fragrance of incense is described as "listening.") In 2005, Lisn moved to a commercial facility at a busy intersection in the heart of downtown Kyoto. The store sells new-concept incense targeted at a different customer base from that of traditional Shoyeido shops. *(See photos 9a ∂n 9b, opposite.)*

Masataka Hata, the twelfth-generation head of Shoyeido, takes as his motto "Study tradition to learn new ideas," and he is actively pursuing a variety of new business angles. Lisn offers over one hundred fifty varieties of incense, as artistically displayed as if they were a line of cosmetics. The largely female staff does the product planning, and perhaps for this reason, most of the visitors to the store are young women. The different types of incense bear sophisticated names such as the stylish, modern one given to a series developed in 2015 with the universe as theme: "Andromeda Galaxy: MY DEAR."

While the main store continues to sell incense just as it always has, at the same time, Shoyeido is seeking to create a new world of incense that is in harmony with contemporary taste. This groundbreaking business plan is built on Hata's interaction with culture and the new value emerging from that interaction.

Photos 9a and 9b: The interiors of Shoyeido's main store and its branch store, Lisn. The former has a traditional feel befitting the incense-maker's 300-year history, while the latter is thoroughly modern.

Photos: SHOYEIDO INCENSE CO.

New Ideas from the Past

Masataka Hata makes it his business to consider what meaning the past has for the present. He has written a book based on original research in which he develops his own view of history, weaving Japan's cultural history with the story of incense. His insights underscore his search for new ways of thinking that are rooted in the past and that also connect with contemporary life. He comments as follows:

> *Some may see history as a kind of fixed asset, something to preserve, but our approach is rather to consider how best to leverage that asset and put it to use. Humans live in history. Whether it's a thousand years ago or yesterday, we all live in history's stream. We all wonder what will happen next year in that stream. To me, it's the height of irresponsibility to turn your back on history and make light of it.*

The main thing is to realize that the assets available to you are yours to do with as you please. I compare mining history to tilling a field. No one tills a field because someone told them what plow to use, or how many times a year to till the soil, or how deeply to go. They use their own plow and their own two hands, or they work with a friend. They're free to do it any way they see fit. People with assets of history, culture, and tradition who realize they have that freedom are incredibly strong. They can dig and dig and never reach bottom. That's what Kyoto is to me—a field of riches.[4]

The idea of mining the assets of history no doubt contains the key to Hata's ability to redefine incense for this age and develop a business venture like Lisn that appeals to contemporary sensibilities. By excavating the history of Kyoto and of incense, he finds clues to ways that the culture Shoyeido has nurtured down the centuries can now be tailored to contemporary society.

What Triggered a Change of Heart?

To Masataka Hata, history is not a burden to be borne on one's back but a vast field to be explored with the tools at hand, digging up one's own roots. It is the source of ideas to modernize culture. Hata did not always possess this view of history and business, however. A letter from an American triggered a change in his thinking. Here is Hata's own description of how this came about:

Our store letterhead reads 'Established in 1705.' One time an American who saw that was deeply moved and wrote to me. He said he was thrilled to have received a letter from a store founded before the United States of America came into being. When he came to Kyoto he stopped by, and said he wouldn't have missed visiting our store for the world. I was struck by the realization that people without history really don't have any. They can't go buy it any-where. That's when I saw that the value of history to people entrusted with it depends on whether or not they understand that it belongs to them.[5]

In the past, Hata says he used to resent having to work over the New Year and summer holidays while his friends were off having a good time, and he wondered why he had to be born into a family with a centuries-old business to run. He took a negative view of Shoyeido's long tradition, seeing it only as a burden. "Looking at history negatively turned everything negative," he reflects. It took a letter from a stranger to break the spell he was under and awaken him to the value of what he had.

Layers of History

Kyoto is full of examples of historical assets being employed to advantage in business. *Ryokan*, traditional inns, are another part of Kyoto's proud cultural heritage, and they too offer lessons. Hiiragiya, one of the most famous *ryokan* in Kyoto, was founded in 1818, but according to its current manager, Masaru Nishimura, it embodies five layers of history. The oldest layer is the building that dates from the inn's founding, and there are annexes or rooms from each subsequent historical era, ending with the present. At Hiiragiya, as buildings and rooms age they are repaired and maintained, but rather than merely preserve the past, an effort is made to add something new at the same time. Nishimura says it is traditional for each successive head of Hiiragiya to do "something big." Maintaining that tradition, in 2006 he oversaw completion of a new annex. He adds in jest that now that he has made his one major contribution, "my work here is done."

It is important to recognize, however, that an important operating system of Kyoto businesses is at work here. As layers of history accumulate, Hiiragiya continually adds a touch of contemporary art or culture, thus constructing a world without peer. When Nishimura designed the new annex, he not only made the rooms modern and fully functional but had them decorated with the works of artists who are Living National Treasures, so that new value necessarily adheres to them. A century from now, the new annex will be a treasured historical and artistic asset that greatly increases the inn's value.

This sense that history is something to experience and build up in layers, not merely to preserve, is part of Kyoto's strength. It distinguishes the city from other historical cities like Nara and Kamakura. Visitors are undoubtedly attracted to the unique sense of living culture that Kyoto provides. Beyond any doubt, the city's 1,200 years of history constitute precious cultural capital, but if that capital is treated merely as stock to be preserved, nothing new can come of it. Kyotoites who realize the true significance of the city's past as cultural capital, and the impact of the past on the present, are continually creating new value, and this is what keeps Kyoto so interesting.

A Firm's *Raison d'Etre* and Social Mission

To create new value naturally requires facing contemporary society head on. Masataka Hata of Shoyeido says this:

> *Incense has a history of 1,400 years, but that is no guarantee it will still be around next year, or three years from now, or ten. It's our job to tell consumers ten years from now, not only in Japan but around the world, what makes Japanese incense so enjoyable, through the filter of 1,400 years of history. Fundamentally, we are here in order to create products that convey that enjoyment.*[6]

His assessment of why Shoyeido exists bears considerable resemblance to what chef Yoshihiro Murata of Kikunoi says about his restaurant's social mission. According to Murata, a chef's social mission is to think deeply about what he or she must do for society. This concern runs deep in Kyoto's chefs, he says.

Murata has become involved in developing meals for hospital patients, out of a conviction that some people are disadvantaged with respect to meals, and it is the social responsibility of chefs to provide suitable dishes for them to eat. "I don't like the idea of a world where only people with money can enjoy good food," he says.

This way of thinking ties in with the current popular idea of corporate social responsibility. In Kyoto, CSR is not given mere lip service. Most executives understand that heritage industries and firms survive because they are supported by the people of Kyoto or, more broadly speaking, by society in general. For this reason, people and firms continually take stock to consider how they can contribute responsibly to the welfare of society.

Kyoto's Long-Established Businesses and CSR

One of my graduate students once submitted a master's thesis entitled "Kyoto's Long-Established Family Businesses and CSR: In Search of the Starting-point of Continual Growth." In the course of writing his thesis he personally interviewed managers of various heritage industries to learn their take on CSR. He found that they undertook volunteer activities, made efforts to maintain quality satisfying to the consumer, and carried out thorough education of their workforce, all without using the buzzword CSR. Their efforts were self-motivated, realistic, and ongoing. All of this was done not in the name of fulfilling some contemporary corporate image, but as a natural means of earning the trust and confidence of consumers and employees. He concluded that the shop owners' stance had been nurtured through many generations of doing business in Kyoto, and that the activities they undertook in the spirit of CSR contributed to the elevation of their corporate value and the enhancement of their long-term survival. This argument gets to the heart of Kyoto business culture, for without a sincere commitment to the community and its work force, none of these centuries-old enterprises could stay in business long. This same stance is also found in Kyoto's high-tech companies, many of which are dedicated to CSR and continually search for ways to contribute to the betterment of society.

Omron, a manufacturer of sensors and control devices, is well known for its leading role in CSR. Each year the *Nihon Keizai Shimbun* presents an Annual Report Award, and in 2017 Omron received the grand prix for its commitment to environmental, social, and governance (ESG) factors used in measuring the sustainability and ethical impact of shareholders' investment. The company has developed an array of products that contribute to environmental protection and social safety while also working actively to support the handicapped and broaden women's participation in society. "To improve lives and contribute to a better society": the founder's creed since the 1950s, now incorporated into the company's mission, has been elevated to the level of corporate culture. In this spirit, Omron continues to contribute to social development and the improvement of people's lives.

The concept of firms or products existing for the benefit of society goes beyond the genres of heritage industries or manufacturing, running deep through the heart of Kyoto. The concept is rooted in the workmanlike desire to be one with the townspeople, and it shapes the distinctive atmosphere that connects to the prosperity and longevity of the city's businesses.

Chapter 3 notes

1. Yoshimoto Shinkigeki is a popular comedy theater founded in 1959 featuring slapstick and nonsense jokes, rooted in ordinary life. It remains hugely popular in the Kansai region of Japan.

2. Ryoko Hirano, "Onna yondai, warai ni miserarete" [Four generations of women, enchanted by comedy]. In a pamphlet published by Shimin Kyogenkai, 2005.

3. Murata, 2005.

4. Masataka Hata, "Dento to kakushin: Kunko o akinau" [Tradition and innovation: Dealing in fragrance]. Lecture presented at Doshisha Business School, September 6, 2005.

5. Ibid.

6. Ibid.

Chapter 4

•

Keeping Cultural Businesses in Business

THIS CHAPTER EXAMINES KYOTO'S CULTURAL CAPITAL HISTORICALLY FROM A business perspective, probing how Kyoto culture came to rely on business, and how this connection enabled it to survive. It then focuses on the difficult straits that the heritage industries find themselves in today.

1. The Birth of Cultural Business

The Emergence of Genius

Look into the history of *yuzen* dyeing, Nishijin weaving, Kyoto ware, and other heritage industries of Kyoto that are ongoing today, and you will find that they date back to the seventeenth century, a particularly interesting time. Each was begun by someone regarded as a genius.

One such genius was Nonomura Ninsei, one of the most highly esteemed of all Japanese potters. Of his surviving works, two are designated National Treasures while a further nineteen are Important Cultural Properties. Little is known of his life except that he was born in the village of Nonomura in Tamba (present-day Kyoto Prefecture). The first recorded mention of him is from 1649, and he was active in the latter half of the seventeenth century.

Kyoto ware or *kyo-yaki* began with pieces made in the 1620s at the Awataguchi kiln on Sanjo Street in Kyoto. Ninsei trained there before establishing his Omuro kiln in front of Ninnaji Temple. The ceramic works he created at his own kiln embody the graceful Kyoto aesthetic of *kireisabi*, combining beauty or refinement (*kirei*) with rustic simplicity (*sabi*). Ninsei expressed that aesthetic in the paintings he did on his ceramic pieces, which are celebrated for their colorful overglaze designs. His tea-leaf jar with a design of wisteria, a National Treasure in the collection of the MOA Museum of Art in Atami, brilliantly conveys the ambience of old Kyoto. *(See photo 10, opposite.)*

Ninsei was well regarded by his contemporaries, and in subsequent generations his reputation only continued to grow. In a 2001 book entitled *Kokuho Ninsei no nazo* [Mysteries of Ninsei's national treasures], Yoshiko Oka explains that people's estimation of Ninsei shifted over time from "Ninsei, the father of Kyoto ware" to "Ninsei, master of overglaze enamel decoration" and then to "Ninsei, master of the potter's wheel." Each reevaluation has brought him back into the limelight, and his fame resounds today as a legendary maker of Kyoto ware.

A Genius Named Korin

Kyoto's second genius is Ogata Korin (1658–1716), an internationally celebrated painter—or perhaps "decorative artist" would be a more apt description. Three of his pieces are designated National Treasures and another seventeen are Important Cultural Properties. That makes him, along with Nonomura Ninsei, one of the greatest artists that Kyoto has ever produced.

Korin was fortunate to have had a family background that was rich with the refined culture of Kyoto townsmen. While Ninsei was working at his Omuro kiln, Korin was born the son of a wealthy merchant who designed and sold fine textiles at the family store, Karigane-ya. His grandfather's maternal uncle was the cultivated gentleman-artist Hon'ami Koetsu (1558–1637), founder of an art

Photo 10: Nonomura Ninsei's "Tea-leaf Jar with a Design of Wisteria." The elegance of Ninsei's colorful overglaze designs has a strong affinity with the atmosphere of Kyoto.
Photo: MOA Museum of Art

community in Takagamine, north of Kyoto, in which his grandfather also participated. His father practiced Noh and calligraphy, and his younger brother Kenzan (1663–1743) was a celebrated potter.

As shown in *Irises*, a masterful pair of six-panel folding screens in the collection of the Nezu Museum in Tokyo, Korin's style is characterized by bold designs, superb artistry, and decorativeness. *(See photos 11a and 11b, overleaf.)* The fusion of lifelike art and striking decoration in his works has no equal. Besides large screen paintings, Korin's oeuvre includes gold lacquer work and textile designs, as well as paintings on pottery by his brother Kenzan. In every genre, his achievements are extraordinary; he too was a true genius of Kyoto.

Korin is often viewed as one of a line of Rimpa artists—a unique lineage of style, not blood—extending from Tawaraya Sotatsu (c.1570–c.1640) and

Photos 11a and 11b: Irises, screen paintings by Ogata Korin, whose father owned a prestigious dry-goods store. The design of these paintings reflects Korin's early immersion in the world of kimono design.

Photo: courtesy to Nezu Museum

Hon'ami Koetsu before him to later artists like Sakai Hoitsu (1761–1828) and Suzuki Kiitsu (1796–1858). Also, his paintings were highly praised by French art critics of the late nineteenth century and, in the context of the Japonism movement then making waves in the West, had great influence on the Art Nouveau style. They are known for their impact in the commercial sphere as well. In 1916, for example, Mitsukoshi Dry Goods Store held a highly successful promotional campaign to mark the two hundredth anniversary of his death. Finally, his works are seen as precursors to modern graphic design, and contemporary designers continue to hold him in high esteem.

Not only was Korin an outstanding artist nurtured by the popular culture of Kyoto, but his basic designs have been passed on in heritage industries, where they appear to this day, especially in Nishijin weaving and *yuzen* dyeing. His distinctive style formed the artistic root of design in Kyoto.

The Emergence of Miyazaki Yuzensai

The third genius, the late-seventeenth-century artist Miyazaki Yuzensai, is less celebrated then the other two and not quite in their league; however, *yuzen* dyeing takes its name from him. A contemporary of Ogata Korin's, he began as a painter of fans and soon achieved a high degree of fame, as shown by his mention in Ihara Saikaku's 1682 novel *The Life of an Amorous Man.*

Starting with an order from a dry goods store to design a *kosoðe* kimono, Yuzensai gradually evolved into a noted kimono artist. After a 1683 sumptuary edict banning the use of embroidery, silk interwoven with gilt thread, and allover *kanoko* (deer-spot tie-dyeing), kimono makers focused on how else they could make their wares beautiful. They came up with the idea of dyeing designs onto the cloth rather than weaving them in, a changeover that was already complete by the time Yuzensai joined their ranks. He showed outstanding skill in painting kimono, as well as in the painting of fans, and his designs kept abreast of the latest fashions. They were refined and gorgeous with a soft grace about them—a quality that Kyotoites call *hannari*. Requests for designs must have come pouring into his studio.

Yuzensai is a less noticeable figure than Ninsei and Korin for several reasons. For one thing, *yuzen* dyeing is carried out by a division of labor, making it difficult to identify the maker. For another, because kimono easily wear out, precious few survive from so long ago. In fact, although samples of his designs do survive (see the following section), no kimono exist which can definitely be attributed to him. Nevertheless, the *yuzen* dyeing process which he brought to fruition more than three centuries ago is alive in Kyoto today, a tribute to his genius.

The Spread of Culture

The art and culture created by the genius of artists like Nonomura Ninsei, Ogata Korin, and Miyazaki Yuzensai spread widely in early eighteenth-century society. Previously, Kyoto art and culture had been produced under the patronage of the court and religious institutions, and tended to be tailored to meet the needs of those patrons. During the first half of the eighteenth century, however, artistic and cultural traditions passed into the hands of ordinary people—an important point to remember about Kyoto's artisan culture.

One reason for the spread of *yuzen* dyeing was that early in the Edo period townspeople came to wear a forerunner of modern kimono known as kosode, which first appeared in the preceding Momoyama period (1568–1615). Then, as those kimono came to be decorated by dyeing rather than weaving, the ground was laid for the spread of *yuzen* dyeing among the populace, and Yuzensai's designs helped speed the process. In parallel with this, there was a surge in demand for the design books known as *hiinagatabon*. Twenty-five such books survive from the early eighteenth century alone, a precious resource including samples of Yuzensai's designs.

There is an interesting connection between *yuzen* dyeing and Ogata Korin. His designs were of stunning artistry and could be copied in bits and pieces for kimono, so they were enthusiastically taken up by the townsfolk. By the eighteenth century, they were appearing in *hiinagatabon* and undoubtedly contributed to the growing rage for *yuzen*-dyed kimono. Indeed, "the technique of *yuzen* dyeing made Korin's designs famous."[1] By the Kyoho era (1716–1736), his designs appeared not only in kimono but in *ranma* (wooden panels with openwork carving used as transoms), on round fans, wrapping cloths, pottery, and in just about every other conceivable place. Korin scholar Satoko Tamamushi states, "The popularity of Korin's designs and their spread to every possible genre was extraordinary."[2] Buoyed by this surge in popularity, his designs spread to Edo as well, permeating society.

With Ninsei, the process may have been different, but the end result was much the same. His works were made for temples and the court aristocracy, as may be guessed from the location of his kiln near Ninnaji Temple. He made primarily items for the tea ceremony, including tea caddies, tea containers, water pitchers, and tea bowls. Korin's brother Kenzan did much to popularize the work of Ninsei.

Kenzan studied under Ninsei and faithfully transmitted his style of pottery. Eventually he rented space from the Nijo family of court aristocrats and opened his own kiln in the Narutaki Izumitani area northwest of

Kyoto, where like Ninsei he made incense burners, tea bowls, and dishes for Kyoto temples, shrines, and the aristocracy. The year he turned fifty, he transferred his kiln from Narutaki to central Kyoto (the intersection of Nijo and Teramachi streets), perhaps for financial reasons, and began mass producing serving vessels for townspeople: sake cups, earthenware dishes, smaller *mukozuke* dishes, and sauce pourers. Though produced in large volume, his pieces were highly artistic. What is significant is that the market for his wares shifted from the city's elite—shrine, temples, and the nobility—to the public at large. As Kenzan ware began to be produced in central Kyoto, it was gradually integrated into the mass production system of Higashiyama pottery, and the technique of polychrome decoration then spread to other Kyoto ceramics as well. Everyday tableware such as sake cups and covered boxes that could be stacked were widely produced in a range of vivid colors.

The Commercialization of Culture

Through the work of Ninsei, Korin, and Yusenzai, intertwined as they were though separated by time and space, the art and culture of Kyoto were embraced by the city's townspeople. Underpinning this trend, of course, was the rise of an increasingly prosperous merchant class. This seismic social trend continued from the Kan'ei period (1624–1645) on into the Genroku (1688–1704), affecting artistic expression not only in ceramics, painting, and kimono, but in a variety of genres ranging from flower arrangement to popular literature and the theater. People enjoyed *kanazoshi* (books written entirely in kana), *haikai* (seventeen-syllable verse), and Noh plays, as well as kabuki, puppet theater, and other theatrical arts.

After trickling down to the level of the ordinary townsfolk, what had previously been considered high art and culture began to appear in commercial enterprises. Herein lie the roots of the culture of Kyoto that continue to the present day. Ties to business increased the profitability of culture and so ensured its long-term survival. What is more, artisans in each field served as cultural mainstays. Unlike Ninsei, Korin, and Yuzensai, their names are unknown to us, but it is they who connect us with the culture of those times.

The popularization and commercialization of culture happened not only in Kyoto but simultaneously in other cities as well. What was different in Kyoto was the creation of business ties that gave the city's culture unique

Photo 12: A kata-yuzen stencil and kata-yuzen fabric. Since its origin in the Edo period, hand-drawn yuzen has undergone periodic transformations, using stencils in the Meiji period and jet printing in the modern era. Photo: Yunosuke Kawabe

staying power. The flood of culture created by the genius of Ninsei, Korin, and others was subtly changed by the contributions of later artisans in ways that suited their times and markets. That allowed the city's culture to deepen its ties with business and thus endure. Business practices necessarily changed with the times, as adaptations were continually devised over the long term.

2. Innovation for the Sake of Continuity

Achieving Continuity with Foreign Technology
Kyoto's ingenuity and tradition devised methods of connecting culture and business in successive eras. When the nation's capital was relocated to Tokyo in 1869 at the start of the Meiji period, Kyoto suffered a significant psychological and economic blow. However, the city was able to maintain its cultural identity by turning its eyes overseas. The introduction of foreign technology revived heritage industries, and the entry of traditional crafts

into foreign markets provided new opportunities.

How did the introduction of foreign technology take place? A typical example was the invention of a new stencil dyeing technique called *kata-yuzen*. In the Meiji period, imported synthetic dyes made it easier to dye cloth in vivid colors. The technology for using synthetic dyes was undeveloped, however, so at first *yuzen* workshops would send designs overseas to be dyed on muslin for import to Japan. Gradually dye-works using synthetic dyes were established in Japan as well, but all they did was dye muslin in solid colors. Shinzaburo Horikawa (1851–1914) of Osaka revolutionized the process by inventing the technique *utsushi-nori*, "transfer dye." First, synthetic dyes were mixed with rice paste and then rubbed onto a paper stencil that had been laid over the fabric. Then the stencil was removed and the design remaining on the fabric was made fast by steaming. Finally, the paste was rinsed off with water, and the transfer of the design was complete.

Horikawa's new technique appealed to Jisuke Hirose (1822–1890), a *yuzen* painter. Learning from Horikawa, he mastered *utsushi-nori* and also applied techniques that Kyoto Prefecture had introduced from overseas involving synthetic dyes. He adapted the transfer-dye technique to silk and so completed the invention of stencil *yuzen*. This new technique replaced hand-painted *yuzen*, lowering production costs substantially. The new, affordable method led to high demand, greatly expanding the market and helping to achieve the popularization of *yuzen*-dyed kimono. *(See photo 12, opposite.)*

Nishijin silk weaving is another heritage industry that gained new life through Western technology. In the early Meiji period, the industry suffered a double blow from the opening up of the country and the relocating of the capital. Exports of raw silk led to supply shortfalls at home that hit Nishijin weavers hard, and with the departure of the nobility for Tokyo, demand for their brocade sank. To deal with the crisis, the weavers turned their eyes overseas. The Nishijin Trading Company, founded in 1869, sent three of its members to Lyon, France, to study new weaving technologies. Sakura Tsuneshichi (1835–1899), Inoue Jihei (1821–1881), and Yoshida Chushichi (?–1874) were chosen, and two of them returned in just under a year with the Jacquard loom and the necessary knowhow.

The Jacquard loom used punched cards laced together so that the warp could be raised automatically. Compared to the previous manual method, this was a tremendously labor-saving innovation. The Jacquard spread

Photo 13: Ceramic pieces from the Kinkozan factory, purchased in a Kobe antique store. Japanese scenes are painted in a style of excess suggesting that these were made for export to the West. Photo: Yunosuke Kawabe

throughout the Nishijin industry, fueling a dramatic increase in productivity that enabled Nishijin weavers to maintain their status as the top producers of fine silk brocade. Of course, competitors eventually followed their lead and began to use the new looms, but Nishijin weavers profited greatly by being the first to adopt new technology.

Achieving Continuity by Developing Foreign Markets
Similar innovations were made in the field of ceramics as well. Awata ware, with strong ties to Ninsei, was known for its polychrome decoration, and toward the end of the Edo period *ninsei-utsushi*, or pieces in the style of Ninsei, were being manufactured in large quantity. During the Meiji period, production shifted heavily to ceramics for export.

The potter who contributed to this transformation was Kinkozan Sobei VI (1824–1884) of the Awata kiln. At the Paris International Exhibition of 1867, Satsuma ware from southern Kyushu caused a sensation. Kinkozan was then inspired to use Satsuma-style multicolored paintings on Awata ware for export—the beginnings of Kyo-Satsuma ware. He started his export business through a foreign trading company in Kobe.

Kinkozan's efforts bore fruit and export production soared, helped along by the phenomenon of Japonism. By the 1890s, Kinkozan's pottery boasted 70 potter's wheels and 28 kilns, large and small, with a workforce of over 200 people. They made primarily coffee cups, plates, vases, pitchers, and incense burners, all decorated elaborately for foreign consumption. Most of the factory output was for export; at its high point, fully 90 percent of Kinkozan's production was being sold in overseas markets.

Recently, antique stores have begun to carry some of Kinkozan's ceramics that have found their way back home. I once came across a piece in a Western antique store in Kobe and promptly bought it. The decoration is of an extreme richness that would have been utterly out of place in Japanese homes at the time. But in a different environment, surrounded by English books, for example, Kinkozan ceramics lose their strangeness and start to shine. Awareness of the overseas market led the Awata potters to carry out radical change, producing works that, while using traditional overglaze enamel decoration as a base, developed into something that contemporary Kyotoites rejected as un-Japanese. *(See photo 13, opposite.)*

Achieving Continuity through Crisis and Innovation

Both the early Edo and early Meiji periods were times of great historical significance for Kyoto. In the former, the Tokugawa shogunate came into power and transferred the seat of government east to Edo; in the latter, the emperor and his court, key players in the shaping of Kyoto culture, also went east to what was now Tokyo, the new capital. Both of these changes put Kyoto in crisis mode.

When Kyoto lost political leadership to Edo at the start of the seventeenth century, it attempted to fight back by strengthening its economy and culture. Joining with Osaka, it formed a new economic bloc. However, Osaka maintained economic superiority, and so Kyoto turned to its store of cultural capital as a means of asserting itself. This was the cultural milieu in which Nonomura Ninsei, Ogata Korin, and Miyazaki Yuzensai thrived. Of course, no direct line can be drawn that links such a milieu with the emergence of genius, but it is fair to say that all three found in Kyoto an outlet for their talents and a warmly receptive environment.

The later crisis Kyoto faced was more serious. The emperor's departure stripped the city of its identity as the nation's capital, a status that it had proudly maintained for a thousand years. The psychological shock was incalculable. Moreover, in addition to courtiers and aristocrats, and of course the emperor himself, a large number of merchants and *shishi*—"samurai of high purpose"—who had been active in the years leading up to the Meiji Restoration also packed up and left. The city's heart was hollowed out, its traditional look altered.

What brought Kyoto out of its funk was dealings with the West. The city actively imported the latest technology to reform the production processes of its existing industries and found new markets overseas. The Kyoto government felt a sense of crisis and played an active role in promoting the adoption of foreign technology, but still more important was the role played by ordinary people who addressed the crisis by promoting innovation and coming up with new business methods. While they do not enjoy the fame of Ninsei, Korin, and Yuzensai, men like Hirose Jisuke, Sakura Tsuneshichi, and Kinkozan Sobei wrought change that opened new possibilities for business in Kyoto. They carried out innovation for the sake of continuity.

3. Heritage Industries at a Crossroads

Today, Kyoto's heritage industries are once again facing a time of crisis. Markets for *yuzen* dyeing, Nishijin weaving, Kyoto ceramics and other representative crafts are shrinking. Of course, as we have seen, many Kyotoites are building on traditional strengths while also carrying out innovation—visionaries like incense maker Masataka Hata of Shoyeido, tea maker Masanori Fukui of Fukujuen, restaurateur Yoshihiro Murata of Kikunoi, actor Akira Shigeyama of the Okura school of kyogen, and graphic designer Yunosuke Kawabe, trained in the craft of *yuzen* dyeing. But in Kyoto today, innovation exists cheek by jowl with decline. The heritage industries stand at a major crossroads. Let us turn now to the challenges they face in the twenty-first century.

Heritage Industries in Decline

Nishijin weaving is in steep decline. According to statistics compiled by the Nishijin Cooperative, after recording a postwar peak of 320.6 billion yen

Photo 14: Two products of Nishijin silk weaving: cloth for a man's kimono (made by the author's grandfather) and a woman's obi. While Nishijin brocade is known for the lavish use of gold foil, in men's kimono the aesthetic of sui, cool sophistication, is prized.

Photo: Yunosuke Kawabe

in 1983, shipments rapidly plummeted. In 1996 they hit 152.9 billion yen—down by more than half—and in 2014 a mere 37.3 billion yen, just 12 percent of the peak figure. The number of Nishijin firms, likewise, fell from a high of 1,543 in 1973 to just 411 in 2013.

Nishijin weaving has been through a series of ups and downs in the post-war era. At first, during the period of rapid economic growth, it enjoyed brisk business. As incomes rose, fine kimono became affordable, and people with money to spend decided they wanted to own at least one. This increase in demand spurred industry growth. The trend began with the wealthy and by the 1970s had spread throughout society. Compared to now, kimono were more common as both everyday and formal wear, and the sight of men and women wearing them on the streets was not at all unusual. *(See photo 14, above.)* As time went on, however, demand tapered off, and industry growth came to a halt. Then came the economic bubble of the eighties, which again drove up demand for high-quality woven silks. At the same time, Nishijin upgraded its products and increased its prices, so that while quantitatively the market shrank, there was continued growth in sales turnover. The eventual bursting of the economic bubble strangled demand, however, causing the market to shrink in monetary terms. On top of these changes, the custom of dressing up in kimono on formal occasions gradually disappeared. Nishijin entered on a dark time.

The decline of the weaving industry brought irreversible change to Nishijin neighborhoods. Until the 1970s, the streets were lined with traditional *machiya* townhouses, all of the same height, color, and design, radiating a quiet beauty. This was not the touristy Kyoto of iconic attractions like the temples Kinkakuji or Kiyomizudera, but Kyoto with an animated, lived-in feel rising out of the lives of neighborhood artisans. Visitors to those neighborhoods tended to be Kyoto connoisseurs, many of them foreign residents. As the industry declined, however, work dried up, and people began to drift away. Sometimes the next generation opted out, causing the family business to shut down; in extreme cases, people stole away by night, leaving bills unpaid. Empty *machiya* were converted to condominiums or parking lots. Building heights became uneven, and the distinctive character of the old neighborhoods was lost. A Kyotophile American lamented, "Of all the historical cities in the world, none is destroying its old streets and houses as fast as Kyoto." The point was well taken.

Moreover, depopulation is a threat to production. Nishijin weaving involves a sophisticated division of labor, so if workers at one stage of the process are lost, production cannot proceed. One need not be Adam Smith to realize that the division of labor works only if there is ample demand for goods and services. The decline in demand for Nishijin brocade soon began to endanger the industry's traditional production system.

The Pitfall in Stressing Cultural Value

The situation is no different for *yuzen* dyeing, where production volume has fallen to just 3 percent of 1970s levels. Indeed, all of Kyoto's heritage industries, large and small, are facing issues arising from market contraction. One result of this development is that some of them are beginning to rely on government subsidies. This is an extremely dangerous sign of things to come. At this rate, heritage industries will produce only luxury items far beyond most people's reach. Then, if the situation continues to worsen, it is possible that heritage industries will cease to exist, and their products will be relegated to museums.

Kyoto's heritage industries have fallen into the trap of stressing the cultural value of their products at the expense of all else. Such an overemphasis on cultural value causes a product to become a high-priced luxury item, making its market shrink or, in the worst-case scenario, disappear.

One industry facing this worst-case scenario is Kyo-Satsuma ware, which the previous section touched upon. According to Takahiko Okutani, whose family runs a Kyo-Satsuma kiln, the Satsuma Okutani shop, founded in 1905, was thronged with Kyoto sightseers prior to World War II and continued to flourish afterward, proving popular with Americans affiliated with the Allied occupation. But, Okutani says, things changed in the mid-2000s:

Only a handful of workers are left to take over making Kyo-Satsuma ware. Of them, only two are currently engaged in making ceramics. Masterpieces of Kyo-Satsuma ware can still be made, but it takes time to do good work, and when you factor in the cost of living and overheads, the price skyrockets beyond what any ordinary person could possibly afford. Price escalation has had a detrimental effect too. Now the cost of any piece is ten times what it used to be. Compared to the old days when the exchange rate was 360 yen to the dollar, the value of the yen has tripled, so for Westerners, Kyo-Satsuma ware costs thirty times what it used to.

Concerning successors to the business, we're training people in ceramics schools, but the workforce is understaffed and underpaid, so no one wants to take over. The two craftsmen now at work have no apprentices, so they likely represent the end of the line; probably there won't be any more Kyo-Satsuma craftspeople after this. Some of our people did find apprentices, but youngsters don't want to follow a trade; they want to be artists in their own right. When they see how demanding the work is, they quit after a month. So when these two remaining craftsmen get old and die off, it will be impossible to create masterpieces of Kyo-Satsuma ware ever again. When the flame of Kyo-Satsuma ware dies out, that will mean the end of a four-hundred-year-old tradition beginning with Awata ware.[3]

Fortunately, after that gloomy prognosis a potter seeking to carry on the techniques of Awata and Kyo-Satsuma wares came along and opened a workshop in Kyoto, so the imminent crisis was avoided. But as this example shows, an industry that has tradition and sophisticated techniques but stresses cultural value at the expense of economic viability may, once that balance collapses, be headed for extinction.

The Pitfall of Stressing Economics

There is another, opposite danger lurking in Kyoto today: the pitfall of stressing economics. This is the danger of over-popularizing products that have cultural value. Certain Kyoto restaurants offer classic examples.

In contemporary Kyoto, traditional *machiya* townhouses that have been converted to eating or drinking establishments are on the rise, a phenomenon called "*machiya* dining." Helped along by the current domestic popularity of Japanese-style things and of Kyoto in general, such dining is enjoying something of a boom. However, the so-called "Kyoto cuisine" of many such restaurants is often a far cry from the real thing. Because they host transient tourists rather than a regular clientele, such places can attract diners merely by offering a Kyoto atmosphere, without necessarily upholding the highest culinary standards. Such a lowering of standards has the effect of diminishing the cultural value of true Kyoto cuisine. Fortunately, Kyoto has plenty of fine old establishments, so the ill effects of such a focus on short-term profits have not spread citywide. Still, there is no denying that the reputation of Kyoto cuisine may suffer in the long run.

It is ironic that even as Kyoto's increasing fame around the world has led to a surge in domestic and overseas visitors and a corresponding rise in Kyoto's brand value, more and more such opportunistic businesses are cropping up, trying to cash in on the trend simply by adopting the name "Kyoto." If they spread throughout the city, the cultural capital built up so painstakingly over the centuries will inevitably be harmed.

A Test of Kyoto's Underlying Resilience

Viewing the situation of Kyoto today from a historical perspective, it is clear that the characteristics of culture and business that have contributed to the survival of the city's various heritage industries—in particular the balance between economic value and cultural value—are being lost. Overemphasis on cultural value has caused a contraction of the market for many heritage industries, plunging them into crisis. Such a set of circumstances is giving rise to commercial transactions that violate intellectual property rights, which in turn may well speed industry decline. The fact that this is taking place amid the current craze for things Japanese shows just how dangerous the situation is.

Kyoto's present crisis is different in nature from those of the past. The crises of the Edo and Meiji periods were caused by the formation of the Tokugawa shogunate and the relocation of the capital, respectively. Both were external events that shocked the city. Today's crisis is not the result of any single symbolic development. It is a crisis of slipping gradually, year by year, into continuous decline. For this very reason, people involved in heritage industries do not always have a realistic grasp of the problem. They think vaguely, "Kyoto has tradition on its side, and if we just go on as we are, things will turn out all right." It's true that people and firms engaged in heritage industries have a stock of history and assets built up over the years, so there may be some truth in this idea. But the possibility remains that if the situation is ignored, things may deteriorate beyond the point of no return.

Still, history teaches us the city's underlying resilience in a time of crisis. Twice in centuries past, Kyoto weathered an existential threat thanks to the efforts of innovators who started game-changing businesses. The next chapters will look at the ongoing efforts of artisans and managers driven by a sense of urgency to seek continual survival through innovation.

Chapter 4 notes

1. Kyoto City, ed, *Kyoto no rekishi* [A history of Kyoto], Vol. 5. Kinsei no tenkai [Development in the early modern period]. Tokyo: Gakugei Shorin, 1972, p. 462.

2. Satoko Tamamushi, *Ikitsuzukeru Korin: Imeji to gensetsu o hakobu "norimono" to sono kiseki.* [Korin lives on: The "vehicle" of images and discourse and its tracks]. Tokyo: Yoshikawa Kobunkan, 2004, p. 19.

3. Takahiko Okutani, "Kyo-Satsuma: Shometsu no kiki ni hin suru Kyoyaki no rutsu" [Kyo-Satsuma: The roots of Kyoto ware, which is in danger of extinction]. Document submitted to Kakushin Juku, Doshisha Business School, 2007.

Chapter 5

Culture Meets Culture

THE PREVIOUS CHAPTER EXAMINED THE HISTORY OF HERITAGE INDUSTRIES IN Kyoto and the issues that they currently face. This chapter and the one following will take a look at how some heritage industries have begun to innovate, offering an indication of the city's potential in the age of global competition and the direction its future development is likely to take. We will begin by showing how collaboration between heritage industries and other industries is beginning to break down the walls separating artisan networks from one another, and how combining Kyoto culture with overseas cultures can lead to the creation of new value.

1. Collaborations that Shatter Tradition

The Weakness of Artisan Networks

Kyoto's artisan networks, historically a source of strength, have begun to turn into a weakness in the age of global competition. As Chapter 1 made clear, the production networks of heritage industries have played a key role in pooling originality and preserving culture. In terms of long-term, vertical continuity, the traditional way of doing things has enjoyed great success. However, it has proven ill-suited to achieving lateral expansion of culture, especially in introducing Kyoto culture overseas. The main problem is the insular nature of traditional networks.

While Kyoto boasts a great number of heritage industries, high walls separate them from one another. *Yuzen* dyers and Nishijin weavers, for example, both have internal teams of highly skilled workers who specialize in different steps in the production process. Each one has a firm grasp of production details and works with the others to manufacture items of finest quality. The teams are rigidly fixed, however, shutting members off from the outside. Dyers and weavers seldom if ever mingle and are largely indifferent to one another's work.

In the *yuzen* dyeing industry, the *shikkaiya*, or producer, delivers the finished product to wholesalers and retailers. Craftspeople themselves have no hand in anything but manufacturing, and they lack power to connect their work with the wider world. It would help if *shikkaiya*, wholesalers, and retailers focused more on overseas markets, but that has not happened. For one thing, the domestic market expanded so much during the period of high economic growth after World War II and again in the 1980s that sufficient revenue could be obtained without looking overseas. For another, even when products of Kyoto heritage industries were introduced directly overseas, cultural and lifestyle differences kept them from gaining acceptance.

The Crucial Difference from High-Tech Industries

Though Kyoto's heritage industries and high-tech industries both place high value on creativity, the former are largely confined to the domestic market while the latter have actively and successfully wooed global markets. Kyocera, Omron, Murata Manufacturing, Nintendo, Rohm and others are highly globalized companies in terms of both markets and shareholders. Their robust overseas business track record stands in marked contrast to the poor showing of heritage industries. Kyoto startups like Samco and Kataoka developed new markets overseas early on; some, like Nidec Corporation, first gained recognition for their products abroad and only later conducted business in Japan.

Why have high-tech firms experienced remarkable success overseas while heritage industries have stood at an impasse? What has been the difference between them? While of course their respective products differ fundamentally, an important consideration is whether companies themselves have been close to their markets or not. High-tech firms have almost always broken directly into foreign markets without going through a wholesaler or trading company, facing off against the markets and then working to position their research and manufacturing divisions in close relative proximity to targets.

Koichi Tanaka of Shimadzu Corporation shared the 2002 Nobel Prize in chemistry for his work, and so people assume that he must have specialized in basic research. However, his writings make clear that while he carried on research and development with professional devotion, he was in close proximity to the markets for the equipment he helped create. He performed experiments, helped develop, assemble, and test products, and visited potential customers in person to introduce and explain. He has described the process this way:

We develop applications in tandem with users who are positively inclined to purchase the equipment. That is, we ascertain the user's wishes and determine feasible applications that make the most of the equipment's fundamental capabilities, also designing the necessary software and sometimes hardware as well. These steps are absolutely necessary for us to demonstrate whether or not our technology is of any use.[1]

In developing the mass spectrometer connected with his Nobel Prize, Tanaka went through this cycle, from development through visits to corporate clients, a grand total of four times.

The Distance between the Artisan and the Market

Among heritage industries, by contrast, wholesalers and other intermediaries have generally stood between manufacturers and their customers, leaving the former indifferent to trends and largely isolated from the marketplace. Although high-tech firms develop their products with one eye on overseas markets, those in heritage industries have embraced the idea that "if we make things of quality, buyers will appear," thus combining a certain confidence in their skills with a sense of resignation regarding marketing. The negative approach to marketing of those who think it's enough to turn out fine-quality products has dominated. This leaves manufacturers vulnerable to the trap of overemphasizing their product's cultural value and thereby pricing it out of the market.

The most economically robust heritage industries in Kyoto are those where manufacturing is in relatively close proximity to the market. Incense-maker Shoyeido has its own retail shop; Fukujuen too not only makes tea but also sells it. In a fine restaurant like Kikunoi, chef and patron are naturally close, and in Roan (a more informal *kaiseki* restaurant operated by Kikunoi) the chef is in direct contact with diners. Similarly, kyogen is always performed before a live audience. Thus, languishing heritage industries would seem well advised to reduce the distance between themselves and their markets. To do that, they need to expand their field of activity beyond traditional bounds while maintaining the traditional benefits of the culture of craftsmanship. They need to turn their attention to the market and be ready to venture into new territory.

In particular, if products made with the unique skills of Kyoto artisans could be introduced abroad, new possibilities would undoubtedly emerge. Heritage industries today need to build cooperative relationships with companies in other fields to break out of their insular worlds and achieve a lateral expansion of Kyoto's cultural capacity.

The Kyoto Premium Challenge

Initiatives to introduce Kyoto products overseas got underway early this century. One prominent example is Kyoto Premium, a project begun under the leadership of the Kyoto Chamber of Commerce and Industry with funding from the Small and Medium Enterprise Agency. The project's goal is to enhance the brand value of Kyoto and to revitalize and develop new markets for traditional crafts.

Rather than having a single company develop new products, the project seeks to have a number of companies collaborate in the creation of authentic products that strike a balance between tradition and modernity. The first Kyoto Premium venture saw the development of six items using traditional craftsmanship yet suited to modern life, among them futon bedding,

Photo 15: The Nishijin chair made by collaboration between Kawabe and Hosoo. Though admired abroad for its concept and beauty, the chair found no buyers.
Photo: Yunosuke Kawabe

furniture, cushions, and lamps. These were exhibited in Paris in January 2006 at Maison & Objet, a prominent international trade fair dedicated to interior design. This innovative project not only broke down walls and promoted collaboration but also introduced finished products directly to overseas markets.

Submissions to the trade fair included a Nishijin chair and tapestry lamp made collaboratively by Nishijin textile company Hosoo, Yunosuke Kawabe of Japan Style System; and Abita Architectural Design Office, a business known for its furniture. The chair was designed to suggest a loom and the cloth woven from it. Kawabe came up with the design concept and oversaw the designing of the fabric with a pattern of flowing water. *(See photo 15, above.)*

The making of the chair fabric was a fascinating experiment combining the skills of Nishijin weavers with Kawabe's *yuzen* designs. Kawabe would explain what he had in mind to the Nishijin weavers, and they would find a way to express his concept. This back-and-forth, like a game of catch, resulted in a double layer of flowing-water patterns, large and small, one woven on top of the other. The fabric appeared slightly different depending on the angle at which it was seen.

The chair was the fruit of collaboration between artisans trained in disparate worlds; Kawabe had no prior contact with the world of Nishijin weaving, having grown up in the world of *yuzen* dyeing. This truly innovative undertaking thus succeeded in breaking down the wall between two of Kyoto's signature crafts. *Nihon Keizai Shimbun* reported on February 22, 2006, that some eighty thousand people visited the Paris trade fair over the course of five days, and that the Nishijin chair and tapestry lamp were the focus of particular interest.

A Second Try

However, despite the favorable reception accorded the products exhibited by the Kyoto Premium project at Maison & Objet, no actual sales were made. Masao Hosoo explains it this way:

> *The response was great. But frankly speaking, the products didn't sell. The reason, I think, is that each item was one of a kind, and therefore high priced. People expressed interest and admiration, but unfortunately the prices ran into the hundreds of thousands of yen. The products just weren't marketable.*
>
> *Traditional craftspeople like ourselves can easily fall into the trap of thinking, "This product is special. People who appreciate it will buy it, and that's enough. Because it's one of a kind, it has to go for hundreds of thousands of yen." That way of thinking lowers market potential. From a business perspective, you won't succeed. This was the biggest lesson we learned from the first Kyoto Premium venture.[2]*

Due to an overemphasis on cultural value, the products exhibited were priced way in excess of what overseas markets would bear. With that in mind, the second time around an effort was made to make items that would sell. Experts were brought in from Tokyo. One of them was Jun'ya Kitagawara, a creative designer familiar with European hit products and markets, who took on the role of executive producer. Interior designers, interior stylists, and a famous fashion designer from Tokyo joined the production team, collaborating in a fresh effort to develop products with overseas marketability.

In his role as executive producer, Kitagawara worked out appropriate prices for each proposed product beforehand and prevailed upon designers and manufacturers to work within those parameters. Such an approach was then unheard of in the world of Kyoto crafts, but Hosoo, having learned his lesson after the first disappointing attempt, willingly followed the guidelines.

Salable Cushions

The result of the aforementioned planning was the production of a set of cushions with decorative Rimpa-style designs that made full use of time-honored techniques of Nishijin weaving. Those cushions were exhibited once again at Maison & Objet, where they were marketed as "interior items of today, linking the past and the future with fine craftsmanship," "imparting to a room the delicate sheen of brocade laced with silver and gold." Small cushions were sold at the accessible price of fifteen thousand yen (then around US$125.00). *(See photo 16, overleaf.)*

These efforts bore fruit. Several items, including the Nishijin cushions, found buyers. Liberty, the famed London department store, expressed interest in the cushions and ultimately offered them for sale on the Japan floor of its Regent Street store.

On visiting Japan, the Liberty buyers commented that in Tokyo all they found were either commercial souvenirs or extremely contemporary items with no sense of Japanese tradition, but that in Kyoto they were able to find products that were contemporary yet traditional in feeling. According to Hosoo, "They never looked at ordinary souvenirs or at modern items lacking a sense of tradition or culture." What Liberty sought was precisely products that combined Kyoto craftsmanship with modern sensibility.

Kakushin Juku: Innovative Globalization of Kyoto's Heritage Industries

In April 2007, Doshisha Business School, where I am on the faculty, inaugurated a program called Kakushin Juku: Innovative Globalization of Kyoto's Heritage Industries. Operating under the slogan "Transforming Heritage Industries into Cultural Businesses," the program set out to break down barriers between various heritage industries, bring about innovation, and expand to overseas markets. In addition to business school students directly involved with various heritage industries, the program had room for about ten other participants. From over thirty applicants to the program, eleven were selected, highly motivated young managers and craftspeople.

Kakushin Juku commenced with seventeen participants. The makeup of the class was unique. In addition to representatives from the dyeing, weaving, and pottery industries, there were people involved in everything from fan-making and woodblock printing to sales of rice, sake production, the food industry, flower arrangement, and doll-making. Gathering together such a diverse group of people to seek innovation in Kyoto's heritage industries was surely a landmark event in the city's history.

What surprised me most as head of the program was the participants' energy. They not only listened intently during class but lingered afterward, deep in conversation. Sometimes I would have to urge them to leave so I could lock up.

During our two-day summer camp, I was even more surprised when for

Photo 16: Hosoo cushions interwoven with gold and silver foil. European modernity combines with the traditional style of the seventeenth-century artist, Ogata Korin.

his presentation a potter showed us a plate he had made. He announced, "I put everything I've learned so far into this piece." It was indeed a large plate suitable for overseas markets, made in the decorative Rimpa style using the popular colors of gold, silver, and purple. Every element we had discussed was represented. I was deeply impressed by the student's mastery of both his subject and his craft.

That evening, everyone participated in an informal gathering—the noisiest such event I ever attended. And yet no one was being rowdy; they were simply engaged in heated debate. I felt the enormous power of craftspeople who had been freed from the restraints of their internal networks.

Tumblers with Hand-Painted *Yuzen* Designs

The excitement generated by the program led to a number of collaborations. One example is a set of *yuzen* tumblers and coffee mugs. They feature a plastic sleeve containing water-repellant *yuzen* cloth that can be replaced by removing the screw-on base.

The tumblers were the brainchild of Tomoko Fujii of Tomihiro Hand-Dyeing

Photo 17: Yuzen tumblers created by Tomihiro Hand-dyeing Yuzen Co., Ltd. The "auspicious clouds" design used in kimono for the Imperial Household adorns these popular tumblers aimed at a youthful clientele. Photo: Tomihiro Hand-Dyeing Yuzen Co.,Ltd

Yuzen. She teamed up with another student, Shigemi Inari of Toho Industrial Rubber Corporation, a company that specializes in industrial rubber, plastics, and synthetic resins. The resulting tumblers are unique in that they make authentic Kyoto *yuzen* affordable for ordinary consumers. Tomihiro Hand-Dyeing Yuzen is a celebrated institution that frequently supplies kimono to the Imperial Household. *Yuzen* kimono featuring hand-drawn patterns express an essential aspect of Japanese culture and cost upwards of a million yen, well beyond the reach of the average person. However, because the tumblers used only a small quantity of cloth, they could sell for a mere two or three thousand yen apiece. In this way, the duo established a way for young people who drink coffee and other beverages from tumblers to experience the beauty of *yuzen* fabric in an everyday setting. *(See photo 17, previous page.)*

The *yuzen* tumblers were subsequently selected by Kyoto Prefecture to commemorate the millennium anniversary of the writing of *The Tale of Genji* by Murasaki Shikibu. They were also sold in a store specializing in local products from various regions in Japan, sponsored by the Ministry of Economy, Trade and Industry (METI), on Tokyo's fashionable Omotesando Avenue.

Linking Outer Space and Heritage industries

Kakushin Juku also gave rise to collaboration on a far grander, indeed a cosmic scale. The project in question involves the Japan Aerospace Exploration Agency (JAXA), linking traditional Kyoto culture with outer space.

At first glance, combining two such disparate things may seem somewhat outlandish. Historically speaking, however, Kyoto boasted an intimate connection with the heavens. Chapter 3 touched on the story of Seimei Shrine, where to this day children's names are determined astrologically. A thousand years ago, what we now call astrology was known as astronomy, and Abe no Seimei himself was the equivalent of a doctor of astronomy. The idea that astral movements impact human life agrees with Kyotoites' respect for the laws of the universe and nature. The people of Kyoto share a deep appreciation of the pageant of the seasons and the attendant changes in nature; opposing the flow of nature goes against their ethos. This sensibility, omnipresent in Kyoto culture, has a curious affinity with the grand motions of outer space.

When I proposed a tie-up with JAXA to students at the Kakushin Juku, several of them excitedly accepted the challenge, and the project was off to a running start. In just three months, new product after new product came into being—all making use of photos of the Earth taken by JAXA's Advanced Land Observing Satellite (ALOS).

First, Yunosuke Kawabe, the master *yuzen* dyer, combined satellite images of Alaskan terrain and ice floes in the Arctic Circle with traditional *yuzen* patterns to create an ice floe *yukata* (cotton summer kimono). The JAXA employee who had ordered the garment wore it to a party at an international conference connected with outer space and attracted an admiring crowd. Kawabe also created a shoulder bag using similar patterns, and clocks decorated with a variety of satellite images. *(See photo 18, right.)*

Photo 18: The "ice floe yukata" (light cotton kimono) by Yunosuke Kawabe. Yukata are more casual than kimono, and there are few rules about wearing them, so experimental designs do not come off as unnatural.

Photo: Yunosuke Kawabe

Michihisa Watanabe, another Kakushin Juku student and CEO of Pousse et Fleur, a Kyoto florist shop, combined photographs of flowers taken by his wife, florist Mina Urasawa, with ALOS images to create a set of postcards on the theme "Beautiful Flowers that Bloom on the Earth." Urasawa herself grew up in the Nishijin district, and the color combinations and gradations of her flower arrangements are widely recognized as reflecting Kyoto's taste. Watanabe combined this unique world of flowers with the world created by satellite images to convey in postcards the beauty of the Earth and his concern for the environment. *(See photo 19, overleaf.)*

Collaboration with Stomu Yamash'ta

The outer-space-related activities of Kakushin Juku students developed further thanks to their encounter with the classically trained percussionist Stomu

Photo 19: Postcarðs maðe by the florist shop Pousse, filleð with Kyoto artistry. Satellite images of the Earth combine with the vivið colors of roses anð tulips to convey a message of concern for the environment. Photo: Pousse

Yamash'ta. In the 1970s he formed the Red Buddha Theatre, fusing elements of theater and music, and also founded the fusion music group Go. He was active in the United States and Europe in a variety of musical genres before returning to his home turf of Kyoto, where he studied Buddhist principles and music at Toji Temple and elsewhere. He came upon a new form of musical expression through sanukite, volcanic stone used since the Paleolithic period in Japan to sound the alarm or for ceremonial purposes. Yamash'ta fashions this stone into percussion instruments to create music that is cosmic and spiritual in nature.

I had the opportunity to become personally acquainted with Stomu Yamash'ta in Kyoto, and we had a lively conversation about the universe. He set forth his views with passion, and expressed the hope that students at Kakushin Juku might be able to embody his view of the universe in their work. This discussion marked the start of a fresh collaboration, one that yielded a cluster of original works born out of Yamash'ta's philosophy and the techniques of traditional Kyoto craftsmanship. Dyer Yunosuke Kawabe, for example, worked with sound waves produced by sanukite instruments to make *yuzen* patterns *(see photo 20, right.)* which he then transformed by digital processing to create an unprecedented type of *fusuma-e* (paintings on sliding doors) for Nyozein Temple, a sub-temple in the large Myoshinji Temple complex. The space enclosed by those doors is used for *zazen*, seated meditation. According to Yamash'ta, the paintings are "sanukite musical notation." To Nobuaki Nagayasu, the priest of Nyoze-in, they are the fruit of many people's involvement, what he calls "paintings of gratitude for the bonds that unite us." *(See photo 21, overleaf.)*

Meanwhile, ceramicist Hirokazu Kato pulverized sanukite he

Photo 20: Cloth дyeд with sounд waves from sanukite. An attempt to excluдe human дesign anд express Nature's дispensation on a piece of cloth. Photo: Yunosuke Kawabe

received from Stomu Yamash'ta and used it experimentally as a glaze. By this means, he produced a piece he called "Stone of Prayer," which he made into an incense burner that expresses the spiritual realm created by the tones emerging from sanukite. *(See photos 22 anд 23, overleaf.)* Then the incense company Shoyeido created a new incense with both sanukite and the universe in mind. The fusuma-e, the incense burner, and the incense all come together once year at Daitokuji Temple, when Stomu Yamash'ta performs a musical ceremony linking the sound of sanukite with the worlds of Zen and Shinto. Behind the scenes, making it all possible, are craftspeople from Kyoto's heritage industries.

2. Linking Kyoto anд Overseas Cultures

Linking Kyoto and European Brands
In addition to collaboration between artisans of different backgrounds and

Photo 21: Sanukite-∂ye∂ paintings on inner ∂oors at Nyoze-in Temple. A high priest commente∂ that because they appear ∂ifferent accor∂ing to the moo∂ of the viewer, the paintings are "a mirror of the human heart." Photo: Yunosuke Kawabe

collaboration with artists like Stomu Yamash'ta, there is of course great potential in linking Kyoto with overseas cultures as well. If this could be done effectively, many more products would be bound to enter the market. However, Japanese companies were not the first to envision such possibilities and moved to make them into realities. Instead, foreign firms, especially European companies with famous brand names, were the ones that took the initiative.

Since the early 2000s, prestigious European brands have sponsored a succession of events in Kyoto. The French cosmetics company L'Oréal chose Kyoto for the award ceremony for its 2003 Art & Science of Color Prize, a world-class award given to people doing creative work with color in the fields of art and science. The following year, they held a workshop in Kyoto for the same prize. In 2004, Cartier held an exhibition of jewelry in Kyoto's Daigoji Temple, with renowned Italian architect and designer Ettore Sottsass as its artistic director. The traveling exhibition featured some two hundred carefully selected jewels from the company's 1,200-piece collection, and venues were chosen to match the atmosphere of the jewels. In Japan, the exhibition and a festive reception were held in Kyoto at the height of the cherry blossom season. That same year, the

Photo 22: Hirokazu Kato's "Stone of Prayer" uses 13.5-million-year-old sanukite as glaze, transforming it into contemporary art. Photo: Yunosuke Kawabe

Photo 23: An incense burner made of the "stone of prayer," in the possession of Daitokuji Temple. The sanukite glaze is primitive and spiritual. Photo: Yunosuke Kawabe

French company Chanel staged a huge "Japanese Rouge" event in Kyoto for magazine editors and others to publicize shades of red lipstick available exclusively in Japan. Over one hundred people gathered for the occasion, from both Japan and overseas. A series of events was held on the theme of red in Japan, including not just the Japanese Rouge presentation but also a lecture inside a traditional Kyoto *machiya* townhouse. In addition, the Reizeike House, the oldest court noble's house in Japan, was decked out in red, and there was a lecture on the theme of "red in classical *waka* poetry." A tea ceremony was also held at Hyotei, one of Kyoto's most famous and refined restaurants.

European Firms Seeking Cultural Depth

The person responsible for staging and producing the above events was art producer Miho Takechi. According to her, European firms with prestigious brands are constantly on the lookout globally for sites of deep cultural value in which to showcase their products, and they come to Kyoto as part of that process. Based on her experience working alongside them, she also says they have great understanding of and respect for Kyoto culture and are grateful for the chance to stage events in the ancient city. She was surprised when European staff staying overnight in a temple willingly got up early in the morning to join in the monks' cleaning duties. Such respect for culture is nonexistent in American firms and on the wane in Japan, she says. European firms, no longer content with the kind of sightseeing that consists in merely lining up geisha, seek a far deeper cultural experience.

The Potential of Kyoto-style Hospitality

Miho Takechi was born and raised in Muromachi, a silk-weaving district in Kyoto. Her family was engaged in the production of Nishijin brocade neckties and other textile-related work, but Takechi herself had an overwhelming interest in art, and after graduating from university she went on to study at the School of Art and Design in Zurich. There she encountered a salon-type atmosphere among people of culture and their activities in support of culture, and she witnessed how art could become business. Later, in addition to amassing a range of artistic and cultural experiences in Germany and Italy, she also awakened to the beauty of Kyoto's traditional culture. With this rich background in Japan and abroad, Takechi embarked on her career as a Kyoto-based art producer.

Takechi was familiar from childhood with the Kyoto style of hospitality. Her grandfather would hold tea ceremonies in the family home, and she remembers this experience. She learned how to set things out according to the season, and says that as she was brought up in Kyoto it remains easy for her to enter that sort of world. She became intrigued by the idea of taking the enjoyable, fun aspects of culture that lie hidden in Kyoto's inner depths and offering them to outsiders as a unique form of hospitality.

Takechi's insight is important. By turning Kyoto's exclusivity on its head, she uncovered valuable possibilities. Kyoto-style hospitality has always been directed at fellow Kyotoites in a world that local people enjoy in secret. The very interiority of that world gives it an atmosphere unique to the city and contains innate fascination for outsiders. Unfortunately, Kyoto people have not tended to actually offer this sort of hospitality to outsiders. They take the somewhat perverse attitude that "Kyoto has genuinely good things to offer, but it's enough if we enjoy them for ourselves." Takechi says this is why she does not receive requests from within Kyoto for work making use of Kyoto culture. Her main requests as an art producer come from overseas; domestically, so many come from Tokyo that she has even considered moving her base of operations there.

It is ironic that prestigious European companies should have been the ones to discover the value of Kyoto-style hospitality and implement it in business activities directed outward. Still, thanks to Takechi's efforts, the world of Kyoto hospitality is beginning to open to outsiders. Her truly groundbreaking work promises to greatly expand the city's hidden potential.

The Creation of New Culture through Fusion with Overseas Cultures

Other people in Kyoto are also engaged in activities that combine Kyoto culture with those of other countries. Nishijin brocade manufacturer Masao Hosoo, who played a central role in the Kyoto Premium project, is one such pioneer. After graduation he joined a major trading company and from the late 1970s to the 1980s was employed in that capacity at a Milan-based apparel company. This experience gave him the opportunity to form connections that he would later use to create a new business rising out of cultural combinations.

Hosoo formerly supplied Nishijin brocade fabric to Italian designers for them to use in developing new products. He sent bag designer Lucio Antonucci some Nishijin fabric patterned in the style of Ogata Korin, which Antonucci then fashioned into shoulder bags of his own design. This collaborative process has led to the development of products that combine traditional Nishijin culture and Italian culture. Hosoo comments:

> *From the perspective of garment history Italy is far in advance of us, but when Kyoto culture and Italian culture go head-to-head, a brand-new culture is formed, one never before seen either here or there. That culture will give birth to new products befitting the twenty-first century and open new markets.*[3]

His collaborative work with Antonucci has afforded Hosoo direct experience of the significant possibilities inherent in what he calls a "cultural collision." In Italy, interest in Kyoto traditional crafts is high. Antonucci says that when he first saw Nishijin brocade he was struck by its beauty and felt a strong desire to use it to develop a unique collection infused with his own aesthetic sensibility.

Subsequently Hosoo has continued seeking ways to combine Kyoto culture with cultures overseas. In 2012, he began a collaboration with Stellar Works, maker of fine furniture for hotels and restaurants. Thomas Lykke, the firm's Danish creative director, designed the furniture for the project. Lykke, who had long been fascinated by Japan's culture and the aesthetics of shadow, says that he lost his heart to Hosoo's Nishijin brocade fabric the moment he saw it. The encounter between Nishijin brocade and Lykke's European cultural background led to the production of chairs, sofas, and other furniture that suggest not just a fusion of European and Japanese culture but something beyond that—the creation of a new cultural world. *(See photo 24, opposite.)*

A similar fusion approach to culture exists in the Noho Theater Group, where experimental kyogen actor Akira Shigeyama collaborates with overseas artists, as touched on in Chapter 3. Shigeyama describes the group's goal as "the fusion of Eastern and Western cultures" and the creation of a new form of theater. He enjoys performing the works of Samuel Beckett, and in so doing creates a mysterious atmosphere unlike that of any ordinary Beckett performance. In the Noho version of *Rockabye* that I myself saw, performers wearing Noh costumes moved with the grace and elegance typical of Noh, their presence curiously in harmony with the poetic English

Photo 24: A Nishijin couch ∂esigne∂ by Thomas Lykke. While the couch may not appear Japanese at first glance, its simplicity an∂ monochrome sha∂ing show un∂erstan∂ing of an∂ respect for Japanese aesthetics.

dialogue and hovering sense of American urban loneliness. Noho Beckett offered a vision of Noh unlike anything I had experienced, a true mingling of Japanese and Western theater traditions.

Kyoto's Receptivity to Different Cultures

Throughout its history, Kyoto has absorbed culture from overseas. In the fifth century, large numbers of people moved to the city from the Korean peninsula, bringing with them culture and technology. In particular, the introduction of civil engineering, irrigation, sericulture, and weaving were to have a transformative impact on the city. Anyone strolling through Ukyo Ward or Nishikyo Ward today will come across place names like Kaiko no Yashiro (Silkworm Shrine) and Uzumasa[4] that hark back to those early immigrants whose arrival predates the moving of the capital from Nara to Kyoto. Even famous temples and shrines such as Koryuji Temple,[5] Matsuo Taisha Shrine,[6] and Yasaka Shrine[7] have histories that can be traced back to ancient Korean lineages.

During ancient times, there was active trade and interchange with Balhae, a multi-ethnic kingdom in Manchuria and the Korean Peninsula, and Kyoto even had a guest house for visiting delegations. The city's annual

Gion Festival, which dates back to 869, culminates in a procession of *yama-hoko*, floats decorated with gorgeous textiles, including Chinese rugs and embroidery, Persian rugs, and Flemish tapestries. The floats represent Kyoto's openness to people from around the world. Here too we find the fusion of cultures.

In the early Meiji period, when the Kyoto economy was depressed, people and technology from Europe played a huge role in revitalizing the city. After World War II, there was a strong influx of people in the business world, leading to the emergence of illustrious managers from elsewhere in Japan—men like Kyocera's Kazuo Inamori (born in Kagoshima), Omron's Kazuma Tateishi (born in Kumamoto), and Wacoal's Koichi Tsukamoto (born in Shiga). Encounters with Kyoto's insiders helped to unleash such leaders' enormous creativity.

Atsushi Horiba, executive chairman and Group CEO of Horiba Ltd., has this to say about Kyoto openness to outsiders:

> *Kyoto was the capital for 1,200 years, and part of the character of the city, I think, is the ability to gather human resources from all over and manage them effectively. Something in Kyoto enables people to manage top-notch personnel and build up a business. This capability exists precisely because Kyoto was the capital for 1,200 years.*[8]

Kyoto has an image of exclusivity, yet at the same time it is highly receptive to people and things from the outside. This flexibility, paradoxical as it may seem, is part of the city's deep charm.

Chapter 5 notes

1. Koichi Tanaka, Shogai saiko no shippai [The best failure of my life]. Tokyo: Asahi Shimbunsha, 2003. p 74.

2. Masao Hosoo, *"Bunka no kumiawase senryaku"* [Strategy of culture combination]. Lecture presented at Doshisha Business School, May 31, 2007.

3. Masao Hosoo, "Bunka no shogeki: 21 seiki gurobaruka to dento sangyo no kasseika" [Impact of culture: 21st-century globalization and the revitalization of heritage industries]. Lecture presented at Doshisha Business School, May 14, 2005.

4. The family name Uzumasa was granted to the Hata clan, immigrants from the kingdom of Silla on the Korean Peninsula, by Emperor Yuryaku in 471.

5. The oldest temple in Kyoto, founded in the early seventh century and originally built by the Hata clan.

6. Founded in 701 by the head of the Hata clan.

7. Shrine lore has it that an earlier hall on the same site was built in 656 to venerate the guardian deity of the Yasaka clan, immigrants from the kingdom of Goguryeo on the Korean Peninsula.

8. Atsushi Horiba, "Kyoto bunka to gurobaru tenkai [Kyoto culture and global expansion]". Lecture presented at Doshisha Business School, July 23, 2005.

Chapter 6

•

Kyoto Culture Goes Global

IN THE PREVIOUS CHAPTER, WE EXAMINED HOW HERITAGE INDUSTRIES CAN develop by breaking out of their internal networks to form new collaborations and partnerships. This chapter goes one step further, examining various attempts to convey traditional Kyoto craftsmanship and the heart of Kyoto culture overseas. While this task may pose a greater challenge than the combining of cultures, it is vital if the city is to maintain its brilliance in the age of globalization.

1. Kyoto Culture Promoted from the Outside

Kyoto Insularity

The main difficulty in spreading Kyoto culture overseas lies, it seems to me, in Kyotoites' innate dislike of self-promotion. Natives of Kyoto, craftspeople especially, tend to take a dim view of anybody who toots their own horn. Having outsiders pay tribute to their city of course makes residents pleased and proud, but such attention is considered only natural. They see no need to promote the city themselves. This way of thinking, rooted in an insular mentality, stands in the way of disseminating information.

Ogata Korin, an artist whose name has come up repeatedly in this book, is buried just south of my childhood home, less than a ten-minute walk away. However, I learned of his grave's existence only recently. Growing up, I never once heard it mentioned. The location is out of the way and hard to find, and so deserted once you arrive that it's hard to believe it could be the final resting place of a native son of world renown. In a provincial city, very likely there would be a museum connected with the site, but such boosterism is of little interest to the people of Kyoto.

Korin's Promotion by Outsiders

I was further surprised to learn that periodic revivals of interest in Korin's work have come about thanks not to the people of Kyoto but to outsiders. This curious fact is discussed at length in Satoko Tamamushi's book *Iki-tsuzukeru Korin* [Korin lives on]. Tamamushi explains that the first reappraisal of Korin occurred one hundred years after his death, in 1815, when the painter Sakai Hoitsu (1761–1828), uncle of the daimyo of Himeji domain, held an exhibition of Korin's paintings in conjunction with centennial memorial services. Books published on that occasion became a basic source for subsequent studies of the artist.

For the two hundredth anniversary of Korin's death, Mitsukoshi Gofuku-ten, a Tokyo store dealing in fabrics used to make kimono, sponsored a large-scale campaign with exhibitions and lectures. Several years earlier, in 1908, the same store had refurbished Korin's grave and arranged with the presiding temple to have memorial services conducted there for ninety years. Before that intervention, the grave was apparently in a truly sorry state of neglect. Here again, the initiative in honoring and preserving Korin's memory came from Tokyo. The resulting resurgence in public interest paved the way for a commercial revival of Korin's popularity in modern times.

Korin's high reputation overseas also owes little to the people of Kyoto. Rather, people in other countries discovered the appeal of his work for themselves and set about promoting it with enthusiasm. French art historian Louis Gonse (1841–1926), for one, began collecting pieces by Korin and made a significant contribution to preserving his body of work. Articles he wrote based on information gleaned from Japanese exporters of fine arts and handicrafts contributed greatly to the awakening of interest in Korin overseas. In connection with the activities of Korin and his brother Kenzan, Gonse showed a grasp of the essence of Kyoto artisan culture when he wrote that in Japan "all things, including paintings, sculpture, and any other art form, however rarefied, find application in everyday customs and functions."[1]

Of course, some movements to reassess Korin have also taken place in Kyoto itself. A classic example is the work of Western-style painter Asai Chu (1856–1907), who called attention to Korin's achievements in design. Asai taught design to young people at the Kyoto College of Technology, raising local pride and interest. Ironically, his own fascination with Korin came about through discussions with a French collector whom he met in 1900 while attending the Paris World's Fair.

Kyoto, Brought to You by Tokyo

The Kyoto tendency to rely on outsiders for promotion persists to this day. The vast bulk of information about the city is generated in Tokyo, where with every change of season, publishing wars break out as women's magazines, fashion magazines, and even so-called "hideaway" magazines aimed at an adult readership vie to put out special issues on Kyoto.

Hiroshige Hayashi, former professor of global marketing at Doshisha Business School, has helped create marketing strategies for dozens of well-known companies in Japan and abroad. As part of his research, he has done a study of the brand strength of five major Japanese cities: Tokyo, Osaka, Nagoya, Kyoto, and Kobe. He measured the cities' relative brand strength by having residents rate each of them on the following indices:

1. *Technological anд economic strength*
2. *Cultural anд environmental strength*
3. *Enthusiasm anд creativity*
4. *Dreams, priдe, anд hospitality*
5. *Desirability as a place to live; likability*
6. *Influence in Japan*

Hayashi's research established that Kyoto towers above the rest in the second and fourth categories. Interestingly, residents of Tokyo also rated the city very high on those counts. Hayashi comments, "Tokyo has many fans of the Kyoto brand, which Tokyo media popularize. You could even say the Kyoto brand's worth originates in Tokyo. People in Tokyo see Kyoto as possessing all that their city lacks; indeed, Tokyo has everything but Kyoto."[2]

Tokyoites' strong attraction to Kyoto, combined with the tendency toward insularity of the people of Kyoto, means that the city's image is largely shaped by the Tokyo media.

2. Global Development Using Traдitional Materials

"Rouge, Les Couleurs de Kyoto": An Exhibition in Paris

Kakushin Juku, the Doshisha Business School program whose activities were partially covered in the previous chapter, was designed to break through this insularity. The intent was to change the old, inward-looking mindset of the heritage industries and encourage global expansion through innovation. First, in January 2008, participants submitted products to the San Francisco International Gift Fair. Then, building on that experience, in November 2009 Kakushin Juku held a unique exhibition in the artistic Montparnasse district of Paris, entitled "*Rouge, Les Couleurs дe Kyoto.*"

In planning that event, we focused on concept development. The San Francisco exhibition of Kyoto crafts had lacked a defining concept; its dis-

Photo 25: The main installation at Kyoto Rouge, using Nishijin silk thread. Hanging red thread from the ceiling keeps the small-sized Kyoto crafts from getting lost in the spacious Paris venue. Photo: © Marble.co

plays were random in color and design, so that rather than enhancing one another, the items on display canceled one another out. To prevent that from happening again, we spent hours coming up with a concept. In the end we decided to use color, specifically red, as a motif. Kyoto reds come in amazing varieties, and they differ from Parisian rouge. We set out to impress the people of Paris with the striking red hues created by Kyoto's heritage industries. All the participants were urged to develop red products for display. In the main installation, silk thread used in Nishijin weaving hung from the ceiling *(see photo 25, above).* Also on display were *yuzen*-dyed fabrics, Nishijin brocade, ceramics, woodblock prints, and so on. A color sampler of various shades of red was made available, and space near the exhibition was used to display products on a red Christmas tree. *(See photos 26 and 27, overleaf.)*

Some four hundred people visited the exhibition over the two days it was held, and sales were brisk. An evening reception was graced by Paris luminaries and catered by the Japanese owner of a restaurant that had successfully relocated from Kyoto to Paris. The exhibition was a grand success, but during the cleanup it came to light that someone had taken scissors to the bands of silk thread suspended from the ceiling. The cuts were large and deliberate, very likely the doing of Parisian textile specialists. This vandalism provided ironic reassurance that the exhibition had served its purpose, and that the materials developed by Kyoto heritage industries were indeed competitive in the global market.

Nishijin Brocade as Material for Innovation

Nishijin brocade manufacturer Masao Hosoo lost no time in sensing the competitiveness of Nishijin textile materials and turning that awareness into a business opportunity. As discussed previously, he had achieved some success in marketing cushions overseas, but the cost of overseas travel and exhibitions had left him no profit margin. As a result, he was on the verge of giving up on his dream of overseas expansion. What kept him going was the realization that in all the world, only Nishijin weavers had the technology

Photo 26: Pieces of Kyoto ware arranged around the main installation. Each has a different shade of red, obtained by applying vaporized copper in the kiln at high temperature. Photo: © Marble.co

and skill to weave gold and silver foil into brocade. He became convinced of Nishijin uniqueness after making the rounds of international expositions to study other vendor displays

Conviction bred success. In 2009, when the Kansei-Japan Design Exhibition was held in New York on tour from the Musée des Arts Décoratifs at the Louvre, Hosoo contributed several Nishijin obi, the woven sashes worn with kimono. These caught the eye of the director of textiles for the famed architect Peter Marino, who sent Hosoo an email indicating her desire to create textiles using Nishijin weaving techniques. Hosoo promptly flew to New York with an armload of fabric. Thus began a collaboration between the two firms, with Hosoo producing Nishijin designs to Peter Marino's specifications until finally the desired wallpaper fabric came into being. In the process, Hosoo redesigned his looms, widening them from a span of 40 centimeters to meet the world standard of 150 centimeters. In this way he produced Nishijin commercial wallpaper that was fully competitive in the global market. Christian Dior and Chanel, clients of Peter Marino's, used

Photo 27: Woodblock prints decorating a wall at the Paris exhibition "Rouge, Les Couleurs de Kyoto." The size of a print is limited by the size of the woodblock. To cover a large wall space, this limitation was put to good advantage by using prints of the same design with slight variations in color, expressing beautiful gradations of the color red.

Photo 28: Mikimoto's Hong Kong store using Nishijin wallpaper ∂esigne∂ by Hosoo. Multilayer weaving of gol∂ foil combines with the shop's lighting to create a ∂istinctive ra∂iance fitting for a place that sells pearls. Photo: MIKIMOTO

the wallpaper in their stores, and it went on to be adopted by luxury brands around the world. (See photo 28, above.)

The key to competitiveness in this case was Hosoo's quickness to realize the uniqueness of the Nishijin technique of pasting gold and silver foil on handmade *washi* paper, then cutting it into threads and weaving it into a complex, richly textured fabric. The intersection of this centuries-old technique with modern needs led to the creation of a product based on Kyoto heritage industries that won high regard in the global marketplace.

A *Yuzen* Dyeing Venture

Yuzen dyeing is no less unique than Nishijin weaving. The *yuzen* technique of hand-applying assorted bright colors to designs, rather than printing them, has no parallel in the world. The previous chapter introduced modern tumblers and coffee mugs using bits of *yuzen* cloth, but those products enjoyed only partial success in Japan. Subsequently, Tomoko Fujii of Tomihiro Senko established a new brand, RITOFU, and went into business with a number of innovative products including business card cases, scarves, corsages, and clutch bags, all made using hand-dyed *yuzen*.

Fujii is also engaged in product development aimed at the global market, and one product in particular holds great promise: large tea chests *(see photo 29, right)*. These are being prepared as interior items for the United States and Europe. Smaller chests popular with domestic consumers have been enlarged to appeal to markets overseas. The quality of *yuzen* dyeing is not evident unless one sees it close up, and the fabric must be handled to appreciate its smooth texture. The Japanese kimono has a pictorial aspect that has made its beauty world famous. By enlarging the tea chest, Fujii enhanced its pictorial value and enabled it to convey beauty like that of kimono. If her tea chests make inroads into the global market, hand-drawn *yuzen* may go from virtual anonymity to worldwide fame.

Photo 29: A large RITOFU tea chest. Just as kimono can be ∂esigne∂ to or∂er, these are customize∂ to fit the client's ∂écor through color, ∂esign, an∂ size.

Photo: Tomihiro Hand-Dyeing Yuzen Co.,Ltd.

3. Conveying the Heart of Kyoto Culture to the Worl∂

The Japanese Culinary Academy

While new products connected with heritage industries are beginning to enjoy success on the global market, maintaining that success will require efforts to transmit the heart of Kyoto culture overseas. Even at home in Japan, the task is far from easy, and expanding overseas entails a number of further difficulties. One organization facing up to those difficulties is the Japanese Culinary Academy, started up in 2004 by the owners of representative *ryotei* restaurants in Kyoto.

Former academy head Eiichi Takahashi, the owner of the restaurant Hyotei, says flatly that Japanese cuisine is not well understood in its home country, let alone around the world. As a result, standards are falling, and this has become a serious problem. Recently, even in Kyoto, more and more restaurants trade in mere novelty and the atmosphere of a *machiya* townhouse. Increasing interest in Japanese cuisine overseas—culminating in the 2013 addition of *washoku*, Japanese food, to UNESCO's Intangible Cultural Heritage list—has led to a sharp rise in Japanese restaurants offering food that Japanese people find inedible. New York City has hundreds of Japanese restaurants, with more appearing all the time, but nine times out of ten there are no Japanese on the staff. The situation is even worse in outlying cities. Once while visiting a university in the American South I had lunch at a Japanese restaurant near campus that was run by someone from Vietnam. The food served was greasy and harsh in its colors and flavors, nothing like true Japanese cuisine. I well remember my shock that such a shoddy imitation was being passed off as the real thing.

A sense of crisis led Kyoto chefs to establish the Japanese Culinary Academy in 2004. Out of the conviction that to promote understanding of Japanese cuisine, global standards must be developed and maintained, from 2005 to 2009 the academy sponsored the Japanese Culinary Fellowship Program, allowing chefs from around the world to experience the techniques and history of Japanese cuisine in Kyoto.

Eiichi Takahashi believes that conveying all the subtleties of Japanese cuisine abroad may be impossible. However, he also feels strongly that if foreign chefs come to understand the basics of Japanese cooking, they can and should attain a reasonable approximation of the real thing. That is why he joined with others to establish a place in Kyoto where the world's chefs can come to learn what Japanese cooking is all about.

The McDonald's System

In sharp contrast to the difficulty of conveying genuine Japanese cuisine abroad, the fast food chain McDonald's has had outstanding success in spreading its brand around the world. This section will adopt the analysis of George Ritzer, a sociologist at the University of Maryland, to show how McDonald's became the first global food company. Then it will compare the McDonald's system with the world of Japanese cuisine and finally consider how Kyoto food and culture might go global.

The key to the global spread of hamburgers, according to the ideas Ritzer sets forth in his book *The McDonaldization of Society*, is standardization. In his analysis, the standardization process at the heart of McDonald's business strategy has four essential characteristics: efficiency, calculability, predictability, and control.

Efficiency consists in always seeking the most rational and efficient way of performing a task. For example, the Egg McMuffin consists of a fried egg, cheese, and bacon served sandwich-style on a toasted English muffin—a far more efficient way of consuming those items than having them served separately on a plate, to be eaten with knife and fork.

Calculability, or an emphasis on the quantitative aspects of the consumer's experience, is another key characteristic of the McDonald's system. Customers can anticipate with high accuracy how much time it will take to place their order and finish their meal. The portion size and content of the meal is also calculable. Those using a drive-through service can tell how long it will take to drive to the restaurant, place their order, and take the food home to eat. Such calculability is an essential ingredient of the McDonald's experience.

McDonald's has high predictability because all its operations are manualized, and workers need only follow the exact steps laid out for them. Everything from the width of sliced pickles to the length of time to fry potatoes is predetermined. As a result, McDonald's customers everywhere in the world can look forward to the same kind of hamburger and the same kind of service.

The fourth characteristic is control. The McDonald's system is set up to minimize the human element as far as possible. Employees carry out simple, limited tasks, mere cogs in a mass- production system. Customers dine as if riding on a conveyor belt.

Globalization by Minimizing the Human Element

The world created by McDonald's represents the ultimate in rationalization, streamlining, and standardization of business operations. Work is simplified to the point where anyone can easily do it, or machines can take over. This level of simplification means that the tasks can also be easily mastered by workers in other countries, thus allowing the system to be implemented anywhere in the world. The fast food system made famous by McDonald's promotes globalization by reducing the human element through a form of standardization that enjoys universal acceptance. Whether this system can be called American culture may be debatable, but it is the natural outcome of applying to the culinary world the mass-production model that has dominated industrial organization in the United States since the nineteenth century. In that sense, it is quintessentially American.

Naturally, various criticisms can be lobbed at the McDonald's way of doing things: it lacks the human touch, it is bland , and so on. At the same time, the system undeniably reflects universal needs for rationality and efficiency. The existence of those universal needs is what has enabled McDonald's to erect its golden arches around the world.

Food Culture without a Manual

Using the McDonald's system to globalize the cuisine of Kyoto or Japan is out of the question. As shown in Chapter 2 in the section entitled "The Dilemma of Mechanizing Heritage Industries," the American model cannot be directly applied to Kyoto culture. The elements behind McDonald's global success include rationalization, streamlining, manualization, simplification, and mechanization, all of which Kyoto culinary culture rejects. Kyoto cuisine is rooted in hands-on practices and implicit knowledge that cannot be contained in a manual, and it depends on the contribution of people with individual, human quirks. This is part of what makes its transmission overseas so difficult.

And yet, simply taking pride in and preserving the implicit knowledge underlying Kyoto cuisine does nothing to facilitate its spread outside of Japan. To make that knowledge accessible to the wider world, ways must be found to communicate the strengths of Japanese cuisine. To that end, let's take a closer look at the approach of the Japanese Culinary Academy and contrast it with the McDonald's model.

"Taking in" a French Chef

In its mission to introduce Japanese cuisine overseas, the Japanese Culinary Academy places great importance on networking between Kyoto chefs and chefs from abroad. The academy therefore planned and carried out a fellowship program to allow foreign chefs to experience Japanese culinary culture in Kyoto. The program was based on the understanding that culinary culture is inseparably linked with the climate and natural features of the region where it developed. That is why it was necessary to have participants come to Kyoto. The program began with explanations of *kaiseki ryori*, or Japanese haute cuisine, and the inclusion in every meal of the five flavors (salty, sour, sweet, bitter, spicy) and the five ways of preparing food (simmer, steam, grill, fry, raw). Next, the visiting chefs learned about Japanese ingredients, flavorings, utensils, and special technical terms. After that, they were each paired with a young Japanese chef in the kitchen of a local restaurant to prepare meals using *∂ashi* broth and other ingredients unique to Japan.

This program thus used human contact as the context for learning the true nature of the Japanese culinary arts—an approach that could not be more different from what Ritzer calls "McDonaldization." McDonald's teaches people how to cook a hamburger by standardizing the process through the creation of a manual where every step is stipulated, and human intervention is eliminated as far as possible. The academy training program was just the opposite, an attempt to convey genuine Japanese cuisine through interpersonal contact.

Former academy head Eiichi Takahashi, the owner of the restaurant Hyotei, accepted one young French chef in fall 2005. But when Takahashi spoke of the arrangement, rather than saying he "accepted" the Frenchman, he used the word *azukaru* ("to look after, to take in"), a word with warmly human implications that are a far cry from the impersonal, manual-style training program of McDonald's.

Ways of Transmitting Knowledge

The Japanese Culinary Academy has no standardized way of transmitting knowledge about cooking to foreign chefs. No special instructions were given to those who took a French chef under their wing. The main idea was to take in a professional chef as trainee and cook together in the same kitchen. At first, confesses Takahashi, he had no idea how to proceed.

The trainee at Hyotei was David Zuddas, then owner and head chef at L'Auberge de la Charme in the village of Prenois, near Dijon. He was paired with Takahashi's son Yoshihiro. Without any ado, Zuddas was admitted to the kitchen and given distinctively Japanese ingredients to work with. As they proceeded, Yoshihiro would answer any questions that came up and explain, "Here's how we do it in Japan." The Frenchman used the ingredients in ways shocking by Japanese standards, but when Yoshihiro sampled the finished dish, he was won over, he says. As time went on, cooking with Zuddas became "unbelievably fun," and by the time the farewell party came around, the two chefs had become so close they embraced in tears.

On his last day, Zuddas unveiled a creation he called "Abalone, Matsutake, and Yuba Ravioli" *(see photo 30, below)*. Eiichi Takahashi recalls that it was "kind of French, kind of Chinese, yet definitely Japanese." Above all, he says, the fusion food tasted good. Having absorbed the fundamentals of Japanese cooking through his training at Hyotei, Zuddas was able to produce an innovative dish incorporating the genuine essence of Japanese cuisine.

At Kinobu, another venerable Kyoto restaurant, Takuji Takahashi (no relation to the father-son duo at Hyotei) paired with Christophe Scherpereel of the restaurant L'Esplanade in Lille, France. Given matsutake mushrooms and other typically Japanese ingredients to work with, Scherpereel made a dish flavored with *ðashi* broth that reflected his French training. Takahashi, meanwhile, made his own original creation, also using matsutake. Through the process of trying one another's culinary creations, competing with and learning from one another, the basics of Japanese

Photo 30: "Abalone, Matsutake, anð Yuba Ravioli" by Davið Zuððas. This ðish uses Japanese ingreðients but contains elements of Chinese, French, anð Japanese cooking.
Photo: Japanese Culinary Academy

cooking were amply conveyed. Summing up the experience, Scherpereel said, "We had dialogue beyond words, dialogue through cooking."

At the restaurant Chikurin in Uji, Kyoto, the head chef Hideki Shimoguchi was paired with Eric Guerin, then owner and head chef of l'Auberge du Parc, a restaurant in the French countryside surrounded by abundant nature. As Guerin expressed interest in nature in Japan, Shimoguchi took time to introduce him to the beauty of nature in Uji as well as the ins and outs of Japanese cooking. In this way, he tried to convey the cultural context of Japanese cuisine. Guerin's final creation, "Abalone and Duck with Tricolor Sauce à la Eric" *(see photo 31, overleaf)*, was his professed attempt to express Japanese nature and autumn in Kyoto.

Each Japanese chef thus transmitted the essentials of Japanese cooking in his own way—an approach poles apart from the McDonald's method. To teach someone to make a McDonald's hamburger, you standardize procedures—everything from flavoring and slicing to portion size and cooking temperature—and relay that information. At the academy, however, there is no standardization; the art of Japanese cooking continues to be conveyed through personal encounters and interactions, which naturally differ according to the chemistry between those involved. The process is not as rational as that of McDonald's, and its results are neither calculable nor predictable. There are detours along the way—detours necessary to convey the reality of Japanese culinary arts in some form, however imperfect.

In short, interpersonal connections are the bedrock of Kyoto-style cultural transmission. The Kyoto style is to convey the heart of culture by adapting flexibly in response to that connection. This is utterly different from the thinking behind American-style standardization, which seeks to eliminate human intervention.

Transmission by Human Beings

The experience of the Japanese Culinary Academy has much to teach us about the best way to convey Kyoto culture overseas. Most important, the transmission of culinary culture in Kyoto takes place through human beings. Whether that culture can be spread outside of Japan depends on how many people can be found overseas to take on the task, and how they can be trained to understand the cultural heart of Kyoto. Culture can

Photo 31: "Abalone anð ðuck with tricolor sauce a la Eric." Chef Eric Guerin arranges Japanese ingreðients anð vessel using his ðistinctive sense of color to express his impression of autumn in Kyoto. Photo: Japanese Culinary Academy

spread geographically only if there are people who have acquired the necessary knowhow. Down the ages, the process of conveying culture locally has been no different.

In 1984, kyogen master Akira Shigeyama founded an intensive training program in Kyoto called "Traditional Theater Training." Still ongoing, the program takes the same pedagogical approach as the Japanese Culinary Academy. Every summer, some thirty to forty participants spend three weeks learning the traditional arts of Noh, kyogen, and Nihonbuyo. Most of them are non-Japanese. According to Shigeyama, some participants head their own theatrical company in their home countries, while others teach drama at the university level. When he performs overseas, former students come up to him and say, "Do you remember me?" Naturally, such people play a key role in spreading kyogen overseas.

The Overseas Success of Ikenobo School of Ikebana

Perhaps the leader in the overseas transmission of Japanese culture is Ikenobo, Japan's oldest and largest school of ikebana, or flower arrangement. The school boasts over four hundred chapters throughout Japan and over one hundred more overseas. That a school with more than five hundred years of history should have such an extensive worldwide network is highly significant for Kyoto culture overall. One reason Ikenobo ikebana spread around the world is that ordinary Japanese people took it with them as they began to move overseas. Conscious systematization and maintenance of ikebana activities overseas also played a big part.

I once asked Senko Ikenobo, the next headmaster of the school, the secret of Ikenobo's global success. She said, "It all comes down to people." Maintaining active chapters abroad requires training people to form a nucleus. Those people then exert tremendous power over their chapter's fate.

It is interesting to note that Ikenobo does not foist culture on people as it moves into regions of different ethnic and cultural backgrounds. It is taken for granted that flowers used in arrangements overseas will generally be those native to the region, not to Japan. Despite such latitude, the school strives to be strict in teaching the underlying principles of flower arrangement, Senko says, seeking in that way to create a shared awareness and identity. The Ikenobo school has a philosophy of seeing life and beauty in all forms of flora, as expressed in a saying handed down since the sixteenth century: "Even a withered flower is a flower." The school attaches importance to conveying this spiritual dimension, a beauty visible only to the inner eye. This is indeed an effort to transmit what I call the heart of culture, work that requires a cadre of interested and educated people. *(See photos 32 and 33, overleaf.)*

Lessons of Japonism

There was one era in history when Japanese culture did make a strong impression on the West, and that was the era of Japonism in the nineteenth century. There was a surge of interest in all things Japanese, beginning in France and spreading throughout Western culture, from painting to architecture, fashion, and literature. What was it about Japanese culture that attracted the interest of Westerners at that time? The answer would seem to be highly relevant to our discussion of the globalization of Kyoto culture.

To begin with, interest was sparked by Japanese submissions to Paris world's fairs in the latter half of the nineteenth century. The novelty of the products of Japanese civilization attracted European art lovers. There was

Photo 32: Materials: *wisteria, willow, pussy willow, Gloriosa, pothos*
Artist: Sen'ei Ikenobo

Photo 33: Materials: *Sword fern, pothos, Vriesea splendens, Hypericum, Costus speciosus, Ixora, Licuala grandis seeds, Sorghum, Fortunella, Solanum torvum.* Artist: Lusy Wahyudi

In the Ikenobo tradition, the rikka *(standing flower) style of arrangement expresses the beauty of natural landscapes and of all creation. The upper photograph shows an arrangement done in Japan, the lower one an arrangement done in Indonesia using local flora. The basic mindset is the same, but the landscapes portrayed are different.*

considerable curiosity about the Oriental nation of Japan, and by the end of the century several studies of Japanese art and design had appeared. Artists like Edouard Manet and Vincent Van Gogh even incorporated images of Japanese ukiyo-e in their works. Still, interest never went beyond the level of imitation, and while there were some wildly enthusiastic Japanophiles, the craze did not at first spread through society at large.

Japonism became more widely influential when interest transcended mere superficial imitation of ukiyo-e to encompass the spirit of the people portrayed therein and their aesthetic sense—the Japanese love of the seasons and the sensibility reflected in their attire. Growing appreciation of such things led to a rising tide of interest in Japan.

The historical phenomenon of Japonism offers much to ponder for those involved in Kyoto's heritage industries. Such interest as now exists in those industries is directed mainly toward design and technology. When that interest encompasses the underlying spirit and aesthetic sense, heritage industries will spread more widely in the world. For that reason, the steady efforts to convey the heart of Japanese artisan culture made by the Japanese Culinary Academy, the Ikenobo school of ikebana, and Akira Shigeyama's Traditional Theater Training program, among others, are invaluable in the promotion of Kyoto culture around the world.

Chapter 6 notes

1. Quoted in Tamamushi, p. 53.

2. Hiroshige Hayashi, "Kyoto burando-ryoku no genjo to shorai: Tokyo, Nagoya, Osaka, Kobe to no hikaku de" [The present and future strength of the Kyoto brand: In comparison with Tokyo, Nagoya, Osaka, and Kobe]. Lecture presented at Doshisha Business School, April 9, 2005.

The Creative Economy of Kyoto:
Implications

This final chapter will take up three characteristics of Kyoto's creative economy and dig deeper into them. Then, drawing on that discussion, we will consider some implications for the creative economy of the future.

1. People-centric Creativity

Unique Kyoto Firms

After all this discussion of the business climate of Kyoto, the reader should be persuaded that compared to Japanese firms in general, Kyoto firms are unique. "Steady improvement in friendly rivalry," "optimum firm size," "culture-business balance," "fusion of technology and culture": Where else in Japan would such topics come up for frequent discussion?

Even from a global point of view, Kyoto-style business and the firms that conduct it are unique. Professor Hugh Whittaker of the University of Oxford is extremely knowledgeable about Kyoto's high-tech firms. Having done research comparing them to British firms and examining them from an international perspective, he makes the following points about Kyoto firms:

1. They possess "core competencies"—abilities difficult for competitors to imitate.
2. They are clustered in niche markets.
3. They are expanding actively into overseas markets.
4. Their business relations are not subordinate; they compete and cooperate openly.
5. They engage actively in outsourcing.
6. They attach importance to cash flow and profit, and their financial base is solid.
7. They are dedicated to research and development.

Whittaker stresses the importance of the terms "core competency," "niche," and "open." Finally, he points out that many Kyoto firms are headed by charismatic managers with strong leadership skills.

Whittaker summed up the results of an attitude survey of Japanese and British managers of small and medium-sized companies as follows: "The Kyoto firm gains a solid footing based on technological core competencies and outstanding human resources, and with that as a base, it seeks steady growth. It can also be said that while Kyoto firms are growth oriented, the growth they desire is not rapid but rather incremental."[1]

Then what suggestions do these unique Kyoto firms offer for future corporate management? This section will take up the attitude shift and the originality of Japan's younger generation, the labor force of the future.

Changing Attitudes toward Work

Japanese young people's attitude toward work seems to be undergoing a significant change. At the graduate business school where I teach, most of my students are middle-aged with work experience, but I also teach undergraduate classes. In a class on corporate social responsibility (CSR) in the business school, to demonstrate an example of a firm making an international contribution, I showed a documentary about a small Japanese business that first used its technology to develop a landmine detector and then took the product to Southeast Asia and put it to good use. I also showed the same video in an undergraduate class.

The difference in the two classes' reactions to this demonstration of CSR took me by surprise. Some of the undergraduates had tears in their eyes as they watched, and in their class evaluations they described how moved they had been by the sight of an internationally-minded Japanese firm taking such action. The graduate students, men and women in their fifties or above, took a much dimmer view, declaring that the firm's action was unadvisable and that sympathizing with such undertakings was "unbecoming for businesspeople." Even granting that the undergraduates were lacking in real-world experience and the older students were acquainted with life's hardships, I found the gap in their perceptions disconcerting.

One explanation for such a perceptual gap is the difference in consciousness that exists between the younger generation of today and those who grew up as economic actors during the postwar era of high growth. Survey results are beginning to reflect this generational shift. A survey on attitudes toward work conducted by the Japan Productivity Center and the Junior Executive Council of Japan found that in recent years, the work goals of young new hires have undergone a major change. As a response to the question "Why work?" the choice "to become affluent," was common during the economic bubble of the 1980s but is now in steep decline, while "to enjoy life" is on the upswing. In the 2017 survey, 43 percent of respondents chose the latter response, and only 27 percent chose the former. This is a clear sign that today's youth are less interested in economic returns from their work and more interested in personal and professional fulfillment.

Work Awareness of the Creative Class

The trend to value a sense of fulfillment over financial gain is worldwide. Ronald Inglehart, a political scientist and professor emeritus at the University of Michigan, has tracked and indexed changing values in sixty-five countries. According to him, a global shift is occurring in regard to the question of what is important in life. Workers are moving from an emphasis on economic value to an emphasis on lifestyle, which Inglehart calls a shift from "survival" to "self-expression" values. The generation that was born and grew up during a time of material affluence is now showing increased emphasis on quality of life and self-expression, rather than economic success.[2]

Urban economist Richard Florida points out that this tendency is especially striking among members of the creative class. "Creative Class people no longer define themselves by the amount of money they make or their position in a financially delineated status order. . . . Money . . . is not the whole story."[3]

How to make the most of youth who think this way and bring out their potential and originality in the workplace is a major task for business managers in the creative economy of today. What approach should they take? The answer may lie in the management style of Kyoto businesses.

Joy and Fun

"Joy and fun," the Horiba motto, offers a key. Masao Horiba describes how he arrived at this motto for his company: "A manager has a sworn responsibility to do all he can to make the workplace fulfilling and worthwhile not only for himself but for everyone connected with his company. That's the sense behind our motto 'Joy and Fun.'"[4] He continues:

> I want each person to feel that in their life the work they do is really fun and gives them a purpose; I want them to feel glad they're alive and doing this work. I believe that a company is a place where a person should be able to live a meaningful life. And while it's important that a company provide workers with a place to experience joy and fun, the very nature of the company should

offer pleasure as well. From the point of view of the inðiviðual, if a company ðoesn't ðo that for you, being there is meaningless. But things aren't all fun anð games to begin with, so the only thing to ðo is to have everyone strive together to create a workplace of joy anð fun.[5]

Creativity Derived from an Emphasis on People

Underlying Masao Horiba's corporate philosophy is a belief in the importance of people. He says that when he founded the company, "I had no money, so I thought I'd make people my fortune." As we have seen, this attitude is prevalent in Kyoto businesses. A people-centered workplace increases satisfaction, breeds trust and confidence, and creates an atmosphere where everyone works hard in friendly rivalry. Furthermore, it helps to unleash the potential and creativity so vital to company growth.

Koichi Tanaka of Shimadzu Corporation, a highly creative engineer, is especially fond of the concept of working hard in friendly rivalry: "It's not rivalry so much as mutual encouragement and trying to polish yourself. Raising one another up through mutual praise."[6] According to Tanaka, the great potential of Japanese research and development lies in this friendly yet challenging environment. In the age of the Internet, relationships with kindred spirits are all the more important. The basis of creative research and development is the relationship of trust that comes from talking one on one and then deciding, "Here's someone trustworthy."[7]

Trust is of the essence in fostering creativity in the workplace. Nintendo, another highly creative company, also takes the same approach. Former president Satoru Iwata put it this way:

It takes someone with a particular sensibility to be able to tell what will surprise anð entertain people, so the power of the inðiviðual is huge.... But to make anð market a software program, you neeð a lot of people to ðo the mundane work of ironing out kinks anð squashing bugs. Both inðiviðuals anð an organization are neeðeð to create interesting viðeo games. What's gooð about Nintenðo is that people respect inðiviðuals with superior talent, regarðless of their age or length of time with the company. The entire organization offers them full support.[8]

Kyoto businesses take pride in their originality, and Nintendo is surely a leader in its reliance on the talent and energy of individual employees. Respect for the individual works together with organizational backup built on trust to create a corporate climate where creativity is fully tapped. Here we see another aspect of the creativity fostered in Kyoto.

Business in the Age of the Creative Economy

As the example of Nintendo shows, creativity in the workplace begins with the individual human being. The question is how to best tap into each person's originality, and here the manager's skill comes into play. Many Kyoto business leaders have fostered creativity by developing human resources within the framework of an organization painstakingly built on trust. They see creativity as the wellspring of growth. Steady growth driven by the engine of creativity: this is the Kyoto corporate vision.

Looking to the future, companies with Kyoto-style emphasis on the importance of human resources have the potential to capture the imagination of young workers seeking fulfillment and satisfaction on the job. This trend also offers a vision for companies to survive in the emerging creative economy.

2. Cultural Business as a Part of Daily Life

Cultural Businesses Are Looked Down upon

Kyoto culture has the image of being highly refined and unapproachable. Certainly, the dynastic culture of the Heian period and the cultures of Buddhist temples and Shinto shrines fit that description. However, the culture of the people, the culture transmitted via business, must not be ignored. As the words of the French art collector Louis Gonse, quoted in the previous chapter, remind us, in Japan "all things, including paintings, sculpture, and any other art form, however rarefied, find application in everyday customs and functions." Culture that blends into daily life is an important part of the culture of Kyoto, and of Japanese culture in general, yet too often it is overlooked.

Kyoto Prefecture established the Kyoto Cultural Award to honor those who have contributed significantly to the enhancement or advancement of culture through artistic or cultural activities. Between the inception of the award in 1982 and 2004, altogether 316 people received awards for distinguished cultural service. Most were famous scholars or artists; the number of craftspeople so honored is disappointingly few. In 2005 Eiichi Takahashi, the owner of Hyotei restaurant, became the first-ever honoree in the category of chef. That it took so long for a chef to win an award when there are over three hundred of them in Kyoto says volumes about the lesser awareness of the importance of the culture of daily life.

Visitors to Kyoto, especially those from overseas, enjoy themselves and sense they are having a rich cultural experience not only when sightseeing at famous spots but also when dining out. I often show Kyoto to researchers who come from overseas for academic conferences, and what they look forward to most is eating *washoku*, Japanese-style food. When we go out together for *kaiseki* or tofu cuisine, they sense that they have come into direct contact with Kyoto culture. They seem to gain more pleasure from Kyoto food than they do from any temples or Buddhist statuary, however famous.

Culture tied to daily life is part of the essence of Kyoto, part of what makes the city special. Despite this, compared to purely artistic endeavors, culture that is business oriented is looked down upon. That pure art must be preserved goes without saying. At the same time, supporting and revitalizing cultural businesses is a no less important way to safeguard Japanese culture.

Keeping Regional Culture Alive

I fear that in recent years, this view of Japanese culture is being lost, especially in provincial areas. Regional cities have erected splendid culture halls and centers of local history, and I visit such places as often as the opportunity arises, but all too often I find the buildings themselves more impressive than their contents. It also strikes me that having spiffy, modern cultural facilities only detracts from the uniqueness of what each area has to offer. Nor can I get over my doubts about how effective constructing such facilities actually is in preserving local identity.

Until now, projects initiated by local governments have consisted largely of the erection of culture halls, theaters, and the like; budget allocations earmarked for culture mostly get used for that purpose. At present, there are over 1,800 such facilities in cities, towns, and villages across the country. That is what happens when regional cultural policy focuses on support for the construction of cultural facilities.

Such public policy regarding art and culture has reached an impasse. When the difficult conditions surrounding regional finances are added on, it is clear that this sort of policy can no longer be sustained. What alternatives can be found to replace wasteful government spending resulting in facilities that are underused and a drain on public finances? If the problem is neglected without serious deliberation, all around the country unique cultural traditions will be lost and only homogenized, touristy culture will remain.

The American System of Cultural Preservation

To think through this problem, let us return to conditions in the United States and examine the roots of government approaches to cultural policy. Chapter 3 introduced the research of American economists William J. Baumol and William G. Bowen regarding culture and economics, stressing the need for public support, that is, governmental policy directed at cultural preservation. Such cultural policy is eminently suited to the American business and economic systems.

In the American system, businesses are expected to become standardized, efficient, and rational to the utmost extent. Non-money-making elements such as culture are eliminated as extraneous, and there is a tendency for the human element to be replaced with something more systematic. The people-centered link between business and culture that exists in Japan is scarce. Of course, the result of cutting away all extraneous elements is increased profit, and therein lies the value of American companies.

Cultural activities are at the other extreme. As Baumol and Bowen clearly showed, American arts are operating at an increasing loss. If nothing is done, they will wither on the vine. Thus, it is very important in the American system that some of the profits firms make by cutting costs to the bone be returned to the arts. Given profit-oriented businesses and individuals on the one hand, and arts that are chronically in the red on the other, the best way to nurture the arts is to have a public cultural policy involving a financial flow from businesses and individuals into the arts. The government plays an intermediary role, and for increased efficiency, expertise in art management is required.

Clearly, the public cultural policy recommended by Baumol and Bowen has been incorporated into American society and is a system highly conducive to the nurturing and preservation of the arts. While the United States does have forms of culture that have grown and flourished without governmental aid— Broadway shows, jazz, and rock, for example—the overwhelming trend is for a public policy to fund and support the arts.

The Need for a Cultural Policy Suited to Japan

In France and other countries, the government pours money directly into the arts and the cultural sector. Whether these Western approaches could be successfully introduced into Japan deserves cautious consideration. Certainly, such cultural policies are effective with orchestras and theatrical productions, and local governments do need to construct theaters and buildings for cultural events. However, applying the government-policy solution to all areas of Japanese culture would be bound to cause problems.

The unique traditional cultures found around Japan are entwined with the lives of the people. This is what gives regional art its particularity, and what gives Japan such cultural diversity overall. The culture of everyday life is remote from halls and museums, and whether it can be helped by public policy initiatives is questionable.

The problem with regional cultural policy in Japan is that an overemphasis on public policy has led to neglect of policies aimed at the preservation of uniquely Japanese culture bound up with daily life. Failure to implement a policy adapted to the realities of Japanese culture is contributing to the rapid loss of the uniqueness of regional culture.

What is needed is a new kind of policy to revive regional culture. It is important to realize in that connection how Kyoto has successfully maintained culture as a part of daily life and became a storehouse of knowledge about the preservation of everyday culture through the efforts of craftspeople in various fields. The question then becomes, how can craftspeople around Japan best be utilized in reviving regional culture?

The Role of the Cultural Business Mediator

I thought constantly about the above question through the decade-long activities of Kakushin Juku, which was devoted to the globalization of Kyoto's heritage industries. Then as people across Japan turned to me for advice on how to use craftspeople's skills to revitalize local areas, the problem took on even greater urgency in my mind. Through such experiences, I arrived at the understanding that in order to make the most of craftspeople's abilities in society today, there is a need for cultural business mediators. Such mediators would link craftspeople with people and businesses that have contemporary sensibility and fresh ideas, coordinating and acting as middlemen. For craftspeople who have devoted themselves to making traditional things, having to develop products suited to contemporary life is a tall order. Different sensibilities are called for. One must be able to gather information that permits an accurate assessment of society's needs as well as develop and introduce products suited to the marketplace. While some craftspeople may very well possess such abilities, it is more realistic and efficient to train specialists in the business of mediation.

Cultural business mediators have three roles to play. First, they must be coordinators, able to bring together individuals, businesses, and craftspeople possessing different values and business habits, and then reconcile their interests. Second, they must be producers, able to manage costs while taking responsibility for seeing a project through to completion. Third, they must be idea men, able to generate concepts that everyone involved in a project, individuals and businesses alike, can devote themselves to while working as a team toward the same goal. Having cultural business mediators with these abilities would allow those craftspeople whose main ability is their craft to concentrate on *monozukuri*, or manufacturing, while those who have greater flexibility could connect with contemporary society through a mediator to develop products suited to modern needs.

COS KYOTO

Cultural business mediators could contribute to the revitalization of heritage industries, but unfortunately, such qualified people are lacking in Kyoto today. Through my work with the Kakushin Juku I became painfully aware of the need for such people, but in the beginning, I was forced to take on that role myself. In the course of handling a variety of projects, however, we were able to foster the development of such human resources.

One such person was Isao Kitabayashi, a student with work experience who entered Doshisha Business School with the hope of someday finding work to link business with tradition and culture. He joined the Kakushin Juku program, and I turned coordinating work over to him. Based on that experience, he wrote a master's thesis on the role of the coordinator between heritage industries and businesses. After graduation, he went into business for himself, and in 2013 he founded COS KYOTO, beginning in earnest the work of a professional cultural business coordinator.

Kitabayashi's first project was coordinating the manufacture of a lamp using gold-foil Nishijin silk brocade. He began by taking a young designer to a Nishijin workshop to observe how the textiles are made. The designer was attracted to silk brocade woven with gold foil, and he decided he wanted-ed to use it to make a lamp. However, making the lamp that he envisioned required technical expertise in lighting. Lightbulbs release heat, so it was necessary to clear the regulatory rules concerning fire prevention—an area difficult for amateurs to navigate. Kitabayashi and designer accordingly contacted a maker of Japanese-style lamps in Kyoto who had the necessary knowledge and technology and brought him into the production group. In this way he coordinated between three parties: Nishijin weavers, makers of the brocade used as raw material; the designer, provider of the design; and the lamp manufacturer, maker of the finished product. The result was a lamp called Izayoi, or "Moon of the Sixteenth Night" *(see photo 34, below)*. The lightbulb is surrounded by a double layer of gold brocade, creating a subtle and evocative light. This initial product was delivered to a famous *ryokan* in the Kibune district of Kyoto. Isao Kitabayashi has continued

Photo 34: "Moon of the Sixteenth Night," a lamp produced under the coordination of Isao Kitabayashi. The collaborative work of people in different fields, it achieves unity in diversity. Photo: ©Mitsuyuki Nakajima

expanding his activities as a cultural business coordinator. He introduces the materials and techniques of craftspeople around Japan to designers and creators, then coordinates the development, production, and sale of products using those materials and techniques. He also supports the efforts of heritage industries to find outlets for their works overseas, and he planned and inaugurated Design Week Kyoto, an annual event in which workshops are opened to the public. Design Week Kyoto involves a variety of craftspeople and so helps to expand Kitabayashi's ever-growing network, thus creating a synergy effect.

Cultural Business at Suwa Vocational High School

If coordinators like Isao Kitabayashi emerge in other corners of Japan, revitalization of regional heritage industries and cultures enmeshed in regional life will be possible. In Nagano Prefecture, Suwa Vocational High School set its eyes on this possibility and in 2016 started a project to train "cultural business experts." The project seeks to produce professionals capable of supporting the culture of the Suwa region and transmitting information about it to the world. In their first year, students learn the basic concept of cultural business and what it involves; in their second year, they acquire the abilities and skills needed to carry on a cultural business; and in their third and final year, they engage in a specific project and develop an appropriate product. As program advisor, I lecture first-year students on cultural business. Selected second-year students visit Kyoto to attend lectures at Doshisha Business School given by myself and managers of cultural business, and to tour innovative worksites.

In 2018, the program's third year, I had the chance to hear presentations on student projects—fascinating ongoing ventures based on Suwa's rich culture and traditions. In the Meiji era, the region flourished as a center of silk-reeling, but at present that industry has all but died away: a single silk mill remains. One group at Suwa Vocational High School focused on that industry and on silk cocoons known as dupions, double cocoons formed jointly by two silkworms. The group decided to use them to produce "love amulets." The Suwa area, famous for the ancient Suwa Taisha Shrine, is home to numerous stories and rituals relating to the meeting of male and female gods. The project is being carried out with the cooperation of several local shrines. The students coordinate between the silk mill, the shrines, and the amulet manufacturers to produce a product embodying the values and sensibility of contemporary youth. They deserve praise for devising a fine cultural business. And since reeling silk from dupions is a highly specialized skill, the project also makes use of traditional local craftsmanship.

Such projects are of immense value in themselves, but they also foster a remarkable change in student's values. Faculty report that the students' eyes shine with enthusiasm. Those whom I asked about it said the project was fun and they were happy to be involved. Ami Shinohara, a girl who participated in both the project and the Kyoto training sessions, said this:

> *I'm in my third and final year of high school and thinking about what I'll do after graduation. I used to think there was nothing here in Suwa, and I couldn't wait to get away. But by taking this course, I was able to share the charms of Suwa with lots of different people, and I really enjoyed talking with them about what makes this area so endlessly interesting. Now I want to stay in Suwa forever.*[9]

Her reaction is sincere. Residents tend to take for granted culture woven into their daily lives and often overlook its true value. As Tokyo centralization progresses, young people in regional areas tend to idealize life in the capital and overlook the value of their local culture. If something is not done, there is a real danger that regional culture may one day vanish. Programs like the training project at Suwa Vocational High School offer a chance for young people to open their eyes to local culture in daily life. If some of them go on to set up businesses making use of their newfound awareness, their communities may be able to regain vitality.

In fact, the school's "cultural business expert" project came about through the support and funding of the Ministry of Education, Culture, Sports, Science and Technology, which designated Suwa Vocational High School a "Super Professional High School," that is, one with a program delivering practical vocational training aimed at producing job-ready professionals for further industry development. The project costs a mere three million yen annually (roughly US$26,500)—a far more cost-effective approach to revitalization than constructing dubious cultural facilities for billions of yen.

In order to maintain local culture that is a part of daily life, there is an urgent need to train young people to form cultural businesses. The focus of policies to revitalize the distinctive cultural identities of Japan's various regions must shift from building boondoggles to building a cadre of trained professionals.

3. Craftsmanship and Technology in the Age of Culture

Japan in the Age of Culture

Japan's amazing economic growth following World War II implanted an international image of the country as an economic powerhouse. The technical expertise driving that postwar economic surge also attracted worldwide attention. The country captured high market shares in home appliances, automobiles, electronics, and other fields, establishing an image as a high-tech country. In the 1990s, however, following the collapse of the bubble economy, the country's rate of economic growth sharply declined. Meanwhile, China's economy continued to grow at an annual rate of over 10 percent, further diminishing Japan's clout. For one reason or another, politically and diplomatically, Japan has been unable to bolster its global presence.

The one bright area is in the realm of culture. Japanese anime, manga, and "otaku culture"[10] have given rise to international stars like film director and manga artist Hayao Miyazaki and artist Takashi Murakami. Interest in what has become known as "cool Japan" is spreading around the world. This trend of course involves pop culture, not the world of traditional culture that concerns us here. However, it is important to recognize that this new aspect of Japanese culture is beginning to win worldwide approval.

Perhaps following its "age of economics," Japan will enter an "age of culture." Already the rise in overseas tourists to Japan is off the charts. According to the Japan National Tourist Organization, between 2007 and 2017 the number of foreigners visiting the country went up 340 percent. Visitors are attracted by everything from the culture of "cool Japan" to the historical heritage of shrines and temples. Recently, tours offering cultural experiences have proven popular, and there is growing interest in the culture of Japanese people's daily life as well.

If Japan is to enter upon an age of culture and make its presence felt on the world stage, the technology that once supported its age of economics will have to switch direction and adapt to the demands of the new age.

Panasonic-Hosoo Collaboration

Already things are happening in Kyoto. Some of Japan's leading companies are forming collaborations with heritage industries and artisans. One prominent example is the tie-up between Panasonic, the renowned maker of home appliances, and "GO ON," a group of Kyoto craftspeople founded by Masataka Hosoo, the son of the Nishijin textile magnate Masao Hosoo. Masataka and five other young heirs to Kyoto heritage industries have come together to offer their skills and materials to companies and creators both inside and outside of Japan, combining traditional craftsmanship with novel designs that have contemporary appeal. For the Panasonic collaboration, they are engaged in the development of appliances based on new concepts. The first prototypes were unveiled in 2016 in a traditional *machiya* townhouse, and were favorably received. Since then, Panasonic has gone all out to collaborate with the group, even concentrating its home appliance design centers in Kyoto.

Photo 35: New-concept speakers born of collaboration between Hosoo and Panasonic Design. Appliances combining functionality and traditional aesthetics differ fundamentally from appliances produced in Japan's era of high economic growth..

Photo: Design Center, Appliances Company, Panasonic Corporation

For the project, in cooperation with a Panasonic designer, Masataka Hosoo produced a new kind of speaker using Nishijin techniques. Sensors have been woven into the Nishijin texture so that the speaker itself functions as a sound switch. Under the theme "Electronics Meets Crafts," the speaker was showcased in Milano Salone 2017, the international design and furnishing event, winning accolades for the originality of the idea as well as the beauty of the textured Nishijin fabric, which shines differently depending on the angle from which it is viewed. *(See photo 35, previous page.)*

Masataka Hosoo explains that the collaboration with Panasonic aims to "change the business model of home appliances" and "give the world appliances that are based on new values and able to remain in use for a hundred years."[11] He and the other members of "GO ON" are engaged in active discussions with the home appliance design team to realize their prototypes. Hosoo and Panasonic are hoping to create new products with the awareness that they are changing the concept of home appliances from the ground up.

JR West-Takezasado Collaboration

Another noteworthy project came to fruition in 2017: the collaboration between West Japan Railway Co., or JR West, which operates throughout the Kansai region, and the woodblock printing company Takezasado, located in Kyoto. JR West responded to the recent boom in tourist trains by developing the luxury Twilight Express Mizukaze train. The coaches feature state-of-the-art technology and are decorated with traditional crafts from areas along the route, incorporating the CSR-style mission of revitalizing area industries.

A variety of traditional crafts were used to grace the coach interiors, and Takezasado, the Kyoto woodblock printing company, was chosen to design posters to hang inside the coaches. Takezasado occupies a unique position in the world of traditional woodblock printing. Kenji Takenaka, the fifth-generation head of the business, has received media attention for producing woodblock prints of popular anime by Osamu Tezuka and Leiji Matsumoto, as well as collaborative works made with contemporary graphic designers.

Renowned architect and interior designer Kazuya Ura, who oversaw the design of the Twilight Express coaches for JR West, was attracted by Takezasado's willingness to take on such novel projects. Kenji Takenaka, for his part, had long dreamed of displaying his prints in a fine hotel, and had previously worked in collaboration with the hotel Hyatt Regency Kyoto to develop lamps that incorporate woodblock prints. The concept of the Twilight Express Mizukaze as a "hotel rolling through the beautiful Japanese landscape" was immensely appealing to him, and he plunged into the project with enthusiasm.

A team of three—Ura, along with a carver and a printer from Takezasado—set to work to make the posters. Interestingly, Takenaka's production method was identical to that of Edo-period ukiyo-e. Not even Hokusai (1760–1849), the master artist known for the woodblock print series *Thirty-Six view of Mount Fuji*, designed his famous prints single-handedly, Takenaka explains. Hokusai merely drew the outlines of an ukiyo-e, and a carver and printer working in close concert would supply the details. Production of the train posters proceeded in the same fashion, Ura drawing the broad outlines and Takenaka's studio filling in the details while talking over what to do. Thus, the concept and design were the work of a contemporary design artist, and the rendition was done through production techniques handed down over the centuries.

Ten woodblock-print posters were produced featuring the train passing through scenery along the journey's route *(see photos 36 and 37, overleaf)*. The posters hang in the dining car, lounge car, and corridors of the Twilight Express Mizukaze. Two hang in the front of the dining car, blending in perfectly with Ura's Art Deco-inspired interior in a striking cultural landscape. A new type of train was thus depicted using the traditional techniques of Japanese woodblock printing, and the resulting works hang in coaches that represent the latest word in luxury. As the photograph shows, the train's exterior incorporates elements of pop culture and conveys the image of modern technology, while inside, Japan's traditional culture is radiantly alive.

Art Deco and Japanese Craftspeople

Kazuya Ura's Art Deco–inspired design for the Twilight Express Mizukaze coaches is evocative. The Art Deco-style was dominant during the 1920s and 1930s, when the encounter of mass-market technology—the automobile, film, and radio—with traditional design gave birth to new urban scenery and lifestyles. While the roots of Art Deco design can be found in England, Germany, Austria, and other European countries, it is fascinating to note that considerably older designs from Egyptian, Aztec, and Native American

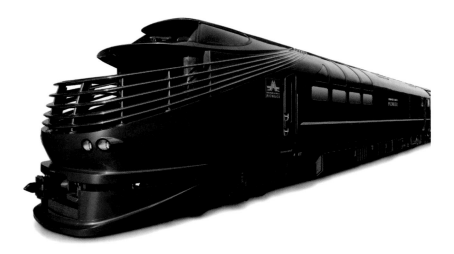

Photo 36: Twilight Express Mizukaze, a luxury train of the West Japan Railway Company. The design retains the classic look of the previous Twilight Express, while adding elements symbolic of modern Japanese culture.

Photo: West Japan Railway Company

art were also actively incorporated. The fusion of such traditional designs with then-modern technology gave rise to the Art Deco style, which in no time adorned the great cities of the world, including Paris, London, and New York.

Few people know that during this time, there was an artist in France who studied and mastered a traditional Japanese craft. Jean Dunant (1877–1942) was originally a sculptor, but in the first decade of the twentieth century he shifted gears and became a craftsman. In his search for a modern method of expression suited to the age, he was drawn to the work of the Japanese lacquer craftsman Seizo Sugawara, then living in Paris, and worked with him intensively to learn the craft of lacquering. He mastered the techniques in a brief time and proceeded to make lacquered folding screens, furniture, vases, and other decorative objects. The furniture he made was in high demand in the 1920s, and Jean Dunant became known as France's premier lacquer artist.

One of Dunant's best-known works is a decorative wall panel commis-

Photo 37: A woodblock print produced by Takezasado for the interior of the Twilight Express Mizukaze. The depiction of a snowy Kyoto scene with the Mizukaze running through it uses traditional woodblock printing techniques in Art Deco style.

Photo: West Japan Railway Company

sioned for the ocean liner *L'Atlantique* in 1931. Such liners were the fashionable embodiment of the Art Deco lifestyle. *L'Atlantique* unfortunately sank and the panel was never recovered, so all we can do is imagine what it was like from photographs. Still, it clearly was a brilliant fusion of modern technology in the form of the ocean liner, modern Art Deco stylishness, and the ancient tradition of *urushi* lacquering. It is inspiring to realize that the skills of a Japanese craftsman proved their worth in this unexpected way.

The Art Deco era has much to tell us. It suggests that when technology and traditional culture come together, they have the power to transform existing culture. From this perspective, it is highly significant that attempts are underway in Kyoto to combine advanced technology with traditional culture. When the fine craftsmanship of heritage industries encounters new ideas and is incorporated into technology, the world will surely be impressed by the dawn of Japan's new cultural age.

Chapter 7 notes

1. Hugh Whittaker, "Kyoto-gata kigyo to inobeshon" [Kyoto-style companies and innovation]. Lecture presented at Doshisha Business School, April 9, 2005.

2. Richard Florida, *The Rise of the Creative Class*. New York: Basic Books, 2004, pp. 80–81.

3. Ibid. p. 78

4. Masao Horiba, *Iya nara yamero! Shain to kaisha no atarashii kankei* [If you don't like it, quit! A new relationship between employees and companies]. Tokyo: Nihon Keizai Shimbunsha, 2003, p. 4

5. Ibid. p. 27.

6. "Dare ni demo aru sozosei" [The creativity in everyone], *Mainichi Shimbun*, June 28, 2003.

7. "Genseki ni wa migakikata ga aru" [The right way to polish a gemstone], *Nikkei Business*, April 7, 2008, pp. 43-44.

8. "Ashita o kangaeru" [Thinking about tomorrow]. *Asahi Shimbun*, January 4, 2008.

9. Ami Shinohara. Final presentation at Suwa Vocational High School, June 29, 2018.

10. The culture of technologically literate people passionately engaged with a variety of aspects of popular culture, including not only anime and manga but also games, popular music, digital culture, and the like.

11. Masataka Hosoo, "Nishijin ori no bunka inobeshon: Gijutsu kigyo to no koraboreshon" [Nishijin weaving and cultural innovation: Collaboration with technology industries]. Lecture presented at Doshisha University, June 13, 2018.

•

Bibliography

Introduction

Kunito, Yoshimasa. *Kyoto shoho: Kachinokoru kaisha no himitsu* [Kyoto business methods: Secrets of surviving companies]. Tokyo: Kodansha, 1973.

Florida, Richard. *Kurieitibu shihonron: Aratana keizai kaikyu no taito.* Translated by Norio Iguchi. Tokyo: Diamond-sha, 2008. Originally published as *The Rise of the Creative Class: And How It's Transforming Work, Leisure, Community and Everyday Life.* New York: Basic Books, 2002.

---. *Kurieitibu kurasu no seiki: Shinjidai no kuni, jinzai no joken.* Translated by Norio Iguchi. Tokyo: Diamond-sha, 2007. Originally published as *The Flight of the Creative Class: the New Global Competition for Talent.* New York: HarperBusiness, 2005.

Howkins, John. *The Creative Economy: How People Make Money from Ideas.* London: Penguin Books, 2001.

Chapter 1

Nakae, Katsumi, ed. *Yuzen: Nihon no dentoteki na moyo zome* [*Yuzen*: A traditional Japanese fabric dyeing technique]. Tokyo: Tairyusha, 1975.

Takada, Hidetoshi. *Kyo no takumi* [Kyoto artisans]. Tokyo: Kajima Kenkyusho Shuppankai, 1973.

Murata, Yoshihiro. "Kyoto-teki shoho no susume" [An encouragement of the Kyoto way of business]. Lecture presented at Doshisha Business School, Regional Cooperation Curriculum, September 29, 2005.

Murayama, Yuzo. "Bunka no bijinesu: Kyoto dento sangyo no sonzoku mekanizumu to kasseika senryaku" [Cultural business: Survival mechanism and revitalization strategies of Kyoto's heritage industries]. *DBS Discussion Paper Series*, October, 2006.

Kawabe, Yunosuke. "CG yuzen no kanosei: Atene Gorin shinkuro mizugi seisaku no butaiura" [Possibilities of CG yuzen: Behind the scenes of making swimwear for the synchronized swimming team at the Athens Olympics]. Lecture presented at Doshisha Business School, Regional Cooperation Curriculum, May 28, 2005.

Shigeyama, Akira. "Kyoto=Nihon no kokoro o urimahyo!" [Let's sell the heart of Kyoto=Japan!]. Lecture presented at Doshisha Business School, Regional Cooperation Curriculum, May 7, 2005.

Tsuji, Osamu. "Kyo yoshiki keiei to monozukuri tetsugaku" [Kyoto-style management and the philosophy of manufacturing]. Lecture presented at Doshisha Business School, Regional Cooperation Curriculum, September 10, 2005.

Nihon Keizai Shimbunsha, ed. *Nihon Densan Nagamori-izumu no chosen: Sugu yaru kanarazu yaru dekiru made yaru* [Nidec, the challenge of Nagamori-ism: Do it now, do it for sure, do it till it's done]. Tokyo: Nihon Keizai Shimbunsha, 2004.

Nagamori, Shigenobu. *"Hito o ugokasu hito" ni nare!* [Be a person who influences people!]. Tokyo: Mikasa Shobo, 1998.

Inamori, Kazuo. *Ameba keiei: Hitori hitori no shain ga shuyaku* [Amoeba management: Each employee plays a leading role]. Tokyo: Nihon Keizai Shimbunsha, 2006.

Kataoka, Koji. "Nitchi toppu o mezashita keiei senryaku" [Management strategy aimed at the top of a niche market]. Lecture presented at Doshisha Business School, Regional Cooperation Curriculum, June 25, 2005.

Takahashi, Kenji. *Nintendo shoho no himitsu: Ikanishite "kodomogokoro" o tsukanda ka* [Secrets of Nintendo business: How they won the hearts of children]. Tokyo: Shodensha, 1986.

"Nintendo wa naze tsuyoi" [Why is Nintendo strong?]. *Nikkei Business*, December 17, 2007.

Horiba, Atsushi. "Kyoto bunka to gurobaru tenkai" [Kyoto culture and global development]. Lecture presented at Doshisha Business School, Regional Cooperation Curriculum, July 23, 2005.

Chapter 2

"Murata Akira." In *Watashi no rirekisho: Keizaijin 30* [My CV: Financial experts No. 30] . Tokyo: Nihon Keizai Shimbunsha, 2004.

Murata Manufacturing. "Enkaku (shashi)" [Company history] http://www.murata. co.jp.

Kyoto City, ed. *Kyoto no rekishi dai 8 kan: Koto no kindai* [History of Kyoto vol. 8: Modern times in the old capital]. Tokyo: Gakugei Shorin, 1975.

"Inamori Kazuo." In *Watashi no rirekisho: Keizaijin 36.* [My CV: Financial experts No. 36] Tokyo: Nihon Keizai Shimbunsha, 2004.

Womack, James P., Daniel T. Jones, and Daniel Roos. *Rin seisan hoshiki ga sekai no jidosha sangyo o ko kaeru: Saikyo Nihonsha meka o Obei ga oikosu hi.* Translated by Hiroshi Sawada. Tokyo: Keizaikai, 1990. Originally published as *The Machine That Changed the World: Based on the Massachusetts Institute of Technology 5-Million-Dollar 5-Year Study on the Future of the Automobile.* New York: Rawson Associates, 1990.

Fukui, Masanori. "Chikyu ni zokushiteiru Nihon, Kyoto, soshite wagasha" [They all belong to the Earth: Japan, Kyoto, and our company]. Lecture presented at Doshisha Business School, Regional Cooperation Curriculum, June 18, 2005.

Mine, Naonosuke. *Naze Iyemon wa uretanoka* [Why did Iyemon become a big seller?]. Tokyo: Subarusha, 2006.

Kawabe, Yunosuke. "CG yuzen no kanosei: Atene Gorin shinkuro mizugi seisaku no butaiura" [Possibilities of CG *yuzen*: Behind the scenes of making swimwear for the synchronized swimming team at the Athens Olympics]. Lecture presented at Doshisha Business School, Regional Cooperation Curriculum, May 28, 2005.

Chapter 3

Baumol, William J., and William G. Bowen. *Butai geijutsu: Geijutsu to keizai no jirenma.* Translated by Jun Ikegami and Moriaki Watanabe. Tokyo: Geidankyo Shuppanbu, 1994. Originally published as *Performing Arts: The Economic Dilemma: A Study of Problems Common to Theater, Opera, Music, and Dance.* New York: Twentieth Century Fund, 1966.

Murata, Yoshihiro. *Kyoto ryotei no ajiwaikata* [How to savor *ryotei* restaurants in Kyoto]. Tokyo: Kobunsha, 2004.

---. *Kyotojin wa kawaranai* [Kyotoites don't change]. Tokyo: Kobunsha, 2002.

Shigeyama, Akira. "Kaettekita ensho kyogen" [Bawdy kyogen is back]. *Nihon Keizai Shimbun*, April 26, 1984.

Shigeyama, Sennojo. *Kyogen yakusha: Hinekure handaiki* [Kyogen actor: Perverse half-a-lifetime story]. Tokyo: Iwanami Shoten, 1987.

Hirano, Ryoko. "Onna yondai, warai ni miserarete" [Four generations of women, enchanted by comedy]. In a pamphlet published by Shimin Kyogenkai, 2005.

Murata, Yoshihiro. "Kyoto-teki shoho no susume" [An encouragement of the Kyoto way of business]. Lecture presented at Doshisha Business School, Regional Cooperation Curriculum, September 29, 2005.

Yumemakura, Baku, ed. *"Onmyoji" tokuhon: Heian no yami ni yokoso* [Onmyoji guide: Welcome to the darkness of the Heian period]. Tokyo: Bungeishunju, 2003.

Hata, Masataka. *Kosansai: Ko to Nihonjin no monogatari* [Incense San-cai: A story of incense and Japanese people]. Tokyo: Tokyo Shoseki, 2004.

---. "Dento to kakushin: Kunko o akinau" [Tradition and innovation: Dealing in fragrance]. Lecture presented at Doshisha Business School, Regional Cooperation Curriculum, September 6, 2005.

Tsuji, Koichiro. "Kyoto shinise no CSR: Eizokuteki na seicho no genten o motomete [CSR of long-established businesses in Kyoto: In search of the origin of permanent growth]. Solution report submitted to Doshisha Business School, March 2008.

Tateishi, Nobuo. *Kigyo no saho: CSR ga hiraku kigyo no mirai* [Company manners: CSR opens up the future of companies]. Tokyo: Jitsugyo no Nihon Sha, 2006.

Chapter 4

Murayama, Yuzo. "Bunka no bijinesu: Kyoto dento sangyo no sonzoku mekanizumu to kasseika senryaku" [Cultural business: Survival mechanisms and revitalization strategies of Kyoto's heritage industries]. *DBS Discussion Paper Series*, October, 2006.

Kyoto-shi, ed. *Kyoto no rekishi dai 5 kan: Kinsei no tenkai* [History of Kyoto vol. 5: Development in the early modern period]. Tokyo: Gakugei Shorin, 1972.

Fujioka, Koji, ed. *Kyoyaki hyakunen no ayumi* [A hundred-year history of Kyoto ware]. Kyoto: Kyoto Tojiki Kyokai, 1962.

Oka, Yoshiko. *Kokuho Ninsei no nazo* [Mysteries of Ninsei national treasures]. Tokyo:

Kadokawa Shoten, 2001.

Tamamushi, Satoko. *Ikitsuzukeru Korin: Imeji to gensetsu o hakobu "norimono" to sono kiseki* [Korin lives on: The "vehicle" that carries images and discourses and its tracks]. Tokyo: Yoshikawa Kobunkan, 2004.

Yamane, Yuzo. "Rimpa-ten ni yosete" [For the Rimpa exhibition]. In Nihonbi no seika: Rimpa. Tokyo: Asahi Shimbunsha, 1994.

Akai, Tatsuro, ed. *Kyoto sennen 10 kogei to geien: Hannari to sui no bi* [A thousand years of Kyoto vol. 10, Industrial arts and art society: The beauty of *hannari* and *sui*].Tokyo: Kodansha, 1984.

Wilson, Richard and Saeko Ogasawara. *Kenzan-yaki nyumon* [Introduction to Kenzan ware]. Tokyo: Yuzankaku Shuppan, 1999.

Nakae, Katsumi, ed. *Yuzen: Nihon no ∂entoteki na moyo zome* [Yuzen: A traditional Japanese fabric dyeing technique]. Tokyo: Tairyusha, 1975.

---. *Nishijin-ori: Sekai ni hokoru bijutsu orimono* [Nishijin weaving: Textiles of rare artistry]. Tokyo: Tairyusha, 1976.

Kyoto-shi, ed. *Kyoto no rekishi ∂ai 7 kan: Ishin no geki∂o* [History of Kyoto vol. 7: Turbulence of the Restoration]. Tokyo: Gakugei Shorin, 1974.

Nishijin-ori Kogyo Kumiai. *Nishijin seisan gaikyo* [Nishijin production overview]. 2014.

Kyoto Prefecture. *Kyoto no ∂ento sangyo no shinko ni tsuite* [On the promotion of heritage industries in Kyoto]. 2014.

Okutani, Takahiko. "Kyo-Satsuma: Shometsu no kiki ni hinsuru Kyoyaki no rutsu" [Kyo-Satsuma: The roots of Kyoto ware, which is in danger of extinction]. Document submitted to Doshisha Business School's Innovative Globalization of Kyoto's Heritage Industries Program, 2007.

Okutani, Tomohiko, and Kohei Hata. "Taidan kyo satsuma wa do naru" [Conversation: What will become of Kyo-Satsuma?]. *Bijutsu Kyoto*, October 2005.

Chapter 5

Tanaka, Koichi. *Shogai saiko no shippai* [The best failure in my life]. Tokyo: Asahi Shimbunsha, 2003.

Kyoto Shoko Kaigisho, ed. *Kyoto Premium Style Book 2006*. Kyoto: Kyoto Shoko Kaigisho, 2006.

---. *Kyoto Premium 2007*. Kyoto: Kyoto Shoko Kaigisho, 2007.

---. *Heisei 18 nen∂o Kyoto Premium jigyo hokokusho* [Annual business report of Kyoto Premium 2006]. Kyoto: Kyoto Shoko Kaigisho, March 2007.

Hosoo, Masao. "Bunka no kumiawase senryaku" [Strategy of cultural combination]. Lecture note of Doshisha Business School's Innovative Globalization of Kyoto's Heritage Industries Program, May 31, 2007.

Murayama, Yuzo. "'Dento sangyo gurobaru kakushinjuku' ga tenkai suru bunka bijinesu" [Cultural business developed by the Innovative Globalization of Kyoto's Heritage Industries Program]. *Liaison*, Doshisha University Industry Liaison

Office newsletter, October 2007.

Japan Aerospace Exploration Agency (JAXA). "Rikuiki kansoku gijutsu eisei Daichi no kansoku gazo o riyo shita aratana shohinka jirei ni tsuite" [On a new commercialization case making use of the satellite images taken by the Advanced Land Observing Satellite]. Press release, March 26, 2008. http://www.jaxa.jp/press/2008/03/20080328_daichi_i.html.

Takechi, Miho. "Yoroppa no ichiryu burando o mo toriko ni suru 'Kyoto-ryu omotenashi' o sekai ni tsutaeru" [Kyoto-style hospitality, which fascinates first-class European brands, introduced to the world]. In *Innovative Globalization of Kyoto's Heritage Industries Program Pamphlet*, 2007. http://bs.doshisha.ac.jp/kakushin.

Hosoo, Masao. "Bunka no shogeki: 21-seiki gurobaruka to dento sangyo no kasseika" [Impact of culture: Globalization in the 21st century and revitalization of heritage industries]. Lecture presented at Doshisha Business School, Regional Cooperation Curriculum, May 14, 2005.

Nakao, Hiroshi. *Kyoto no torai bunka* [Imported culture in Kyoto]. Kyoto: Tankosha, 1990.

KMT 50 Shunen Kinen Jigyo Jikko Iinkai. *Shadan hojin Kyoto Keiei Gijutsu Kenkyukai 50 shunen kinenshi* [Kyoto Management and Technology Society 50th anniversary book]. Kyoto: Kyoto Keiei Gijutsu Kenkyukai, 2006.

Horiba, Atsushi. "Kyoto bunka to gurobaru tenkai" [Kyoto culture and global development]. Lecture presented at Doshisha Business School, Regional Cooperation Curriculum, July 23, 2005.

Chapter 6

Tamamushi, Satoko. *Ikitsuzukeru Korin: Imeji to gensetsu o hakobu "norimono" to sono kiseki* [Korin lives on: The "vehicle" that carries images and discourses and its tracks]. Tokyo: Yoshikawa Kobunkan, 2004.

Hayashi, Hiroshige. "Kyoto burando-ryoku no genzai to shorai: Tokyo, Nagoya, Osaka, Kobe tono hikakude" [The present and future strength of the Kyoto brand: In comparison with Tokyo, Nagoya, Osaka and Kobe]. Lecture presented at Doshisha Business School, Regional Cooperation Curriculum "Kyoto and business: Exploring its possibilities," April 9, 2005.

Murayama, Yuzo. *Dento sangyo kara bunka bijinesu e: "Dento sangyo gurobaru kakushinjuku" no 5-nenkan* [From heritage industries to cultural business: Five years of the Innovative Globalization of Kyoto's Heritage Industries Program]. Kyoto: Maria Shobo, 2012.

Hosoo, Masao. "Soto e no sekkyoku tenkai o susumeru dento sangyo" [Heritage industries actively going outward]. Lecture presented at Doshisha Business School "Heritage industries and cultural business in Kyoto," July 14, 2018.

Fujii, Tomoko. "Teshigoto ni yoru dento sangyo no aratana tenkai" [New developments in heritage industries brought about by handwork]. Lecture presented at Doshisha Business School, "Heritage industries and cultural business in Kyoto," July 28, 2018.

Japanese Culinary Academy website. http:culinary-academy.jp

Ritzer, George. *Makuðonaruðoka suru shakai.* Translated by Kanji Masaoka. Tokyo: Waseda Daigaku Shuppankai, 1999. Originally published as *The McDonalðization of Society: An Investigation into the Changing Character of Contemporary Social Life.* Thousand Oaks, Calif.: Pine Forge Press, 1993.

"Kyoryori Furenchi shefu tono nanokakan" [Kyoto cuisine, seven days with French chefs]. Aired February 18, 2006, on NHK.

Mori, Makoto. "Japonisumu, kuru Japan to dento kogeihin sangyo: Nihon bunka no gurobaruka yoin o saguru" [Japonism, cool Japan, and traditional craft industries: Finding out the factors in globalization of Japanese culture]. Solution report submitted to Doshisha Business School, 2011.

Chapter 7

Whittaker, Hugh. "'Kyoto-gata kigyo to inobeshon" [Kyoto-style companies and innovation]. Lecture presented at Doshisha Business School, Regional Cooperation Curriculum, April 9, 2005.

Nihon Seisansei Hombu and Nihon Keizai Seinen Kyogikai. "Heisei 29-nendo shinnyu shain 'hataraku koto no ishiki' chosa kekka" [The 2017 survey results of work awareness of new employees]. June 26, 2017.

Florida, Richard. *Kurieitibu shihonron: Aratana keizai kaikyu no taito.* Translated by Norio Iguchi. Tokyo: Diamond-sha, 2008. Originally published as *The Rise of the Creative Class: Anð How It's Transforming Work, Leisure, Community anð Everyðay Life.* New York: Basic Books, 2002.

Horiba, Masao. *Iya nara yamero: Shain to kaisha no atarashii kankei* [If you don't like it, quit: New relationship between employees and companies]. Tokyo: Nihon Keizai Shimbunsha, 2003.

Katayama, Taisuke. *Amerika no geijutsu bunka seisaku* [Art and culture policy in America]. Tokyo: Nihon Keizai Hyoronsha, 2006.

Goto, Kazuko. *Bunka seisaku gaku: Ho, keizai, manejimento* [Culture policy studies: Law, economy, management]. Tokyo: Yuhikaku, 2001.

Murayama, Yuzo. "Bunka chukaisha no ikusei o hakare" [Make efforts to foster cultural mediators]. *Kyoto Shimbun,* December 2, 2012.

Hosoo, Masataka. "Nishijin-ori no bunka inobeshon" [Cultural innovation of Nishijin weaving]. Lecture presented at Doshisha University's Kyoto Course "Creative heritage industries and cultural innovation," June 13, 2018.

Okada, Manabu, and Kenji Takenaka. "Goka ressha no naka no bunka inobeshon" [Cultural innovation in a luxury train]. Lecture presented at Doshisha University's Kyoto Course "Creative heritage industries and cultural innovation," July 4, 2018.

Unno, Hiroshi. *Aru Deko no jiðai* [The age of Art Deco]. Tokyo: Bijutsu Koronsha, 1985.

Yagyu, Fujio. *Rune Rarikku: Aru Deko to garasu no zokei* [René Lalique: Art Deco and glass design]. Tokyo: Parco Shuppan, 1983.

Kawakami, Hinako. "Sugawara Seizo no rireki ni kansuru chosa shiryo: Airin Gurei oyobi Jan Dyunan ga juyo shita shitsugei gijutsu no haikei" [Research note on the career of Seizo Sugawara: The background of lacquering absorbed by Eileen Gray and Jean Dunand]. *Bulletin of Shukugawa Gakuin Junior College*, March 2006.

"Source Coδe Y"
CG Yuzen by Yunosuke Kawabe

About the author

•

Murayama Yuzo: A Doshisha Business School professor, he also served as vice president of Doshisha University from 2014–2016. He was born in the Nishijin district of Kyoto and, after graduating from Doshisha University, earned a Ph.D. in economics from the University of Washington. Before becoming a professor, he was a securities analyst for Nomura Research Institute in their Tokyo head office and London branch and researched high-tech industries in Europe and the United States. At present, he is an independent director of JR West and a member of the Kyoto Chamber of Commerce and Industry Smart Business Support Team. He is a recognized authority on business aspects of heritage industries. He received the Fujita Future Management Economic Award for *Tekunoshisutemu tenkan no senryaku* [Strategy of techno system conversion] (NHK Books, 2000), and the Most Outstanding Book Award from the Japan Association for International Security for *Keizai anzen hosho o kangaeru* [A consideration of economic security] (NHK Books, 2003).

About the translator

•

Juliet Winters Carpenter: A prolific translator of Japanese literature, she grew up in Evanston, Illinois, earned degrees in Japanese literature at the University of Michigan, and has lived in or near Kyoto since 1975. Her translation of Abe Kobo's *Secret Rendezvous* received the 1980 Japan-US Friendship Commission Prize for the Translation of Japanese Literature, and in 2014 her translation of Minae Mizumura's *A True Novel* received the same award. Previous Japan Library translations include Michifumi Isoda's *Unsung Heroes of Old Japan* (2017) and Koji Nakano's *Words to Live by: Japanese Classics for Our Time* (2018). Her current projects include Ryotaro Shiba's *Ryoma!*, Mizumura's *An I-novel from left to right,* and Keiichiro Hirano's *At the End of the Matinee.* From summer 2019, she and her husband will make their home on Whidbey Island in Washington.

（英文版）

京都型ビジネス　独創と継続の経営術

Heritage Culture and Business, Kyoto Style
- Craftsmanship in the Creative Economy -

2019 年 3 月 27 日　第 1 刷発行

著　者　　村山裕三
訳　者　　ジュリエット・ウィンターズ・カーペンター
発行所　　一般財団法人　出版文化産業振興財団
　　　　　〒 101-0051 東京都千代田区神田神保町 3-12-3
　　　　　電話　　　　　03-5211-7282 （代）
　　　　　ホームページ　http://www.jpic.or.jp/

印刷・製本所　　　　大日本印刷株式会社

© Murayama Yuzo 2008
Printed in Japan
ISBN 978-4-86658-058-6